Cornelia Hahn Oberlander on Pedagogical Playgrounds

T0283370

Cornelia Hahn Oberlander on Pedagogical Playgrounds

With an introduction by Jane Mah Hutton

Concordia University Press
Canadian Centre for Architecture
Montreal

Introduction by Jane Mah Hutton

Texts by Cornelia Hahn Oberlander

Cornelia Hahn Oberlander's Curriculum for Play

Jane Mah Hutton

The list below is drawn from the archive of landscape architect Cornelia Hahn Oberlander. The lecture notes, office documents, and letters found in the Cornelia Hahn Oberlander fonds at the Canadian Centre for Architecture are peppered with such lists. Some are the bulleted talking points of a well-organized and accomplished speaker, while others are design specifications to direct a playground construction. In the study of early writing cultures, anthropologist Jack Goody identifies three major types of lists: inventories of elements, "shopping lists" of future actions, and lexical lists which define terms.[1]

1   JUMPING from high places; from object to object[2]

2   CARING FOR ANIMALS—ducks, rabbits, hamsters, birds, dogs ...

3   OBSERVING NATURE—tadpoles developing, blackberries ripening, caterpillars crawling, waves lapping ...

4   help give us a stronger spiritual base

5   sharpen our abilities to communicate effectively and reflect the social graces

6   aid body development, movement, and motor co-ordination

7   sand box

8   water-play area

9   rocking boat

10   left-over lumber ends from construction sites donated regularly by builders in the community

11   (hammers, saws, nails) choose the best and most suitable in size; have sufficient in number

12   old car tires

13   You can sift it through your fingers

14   You can eat it

15   You can use it to shape cakes for an imaginary birthday party

Many of Hahn Oberlander's lists seem to be both inventory and action plan at once. One document, titled "Children Like ..." typed on two yellow pages, is a list of twenty-two things that children like—a useful inventory for a landscape architecture office to activate through design. Next to each of the listed items are collaged black and white photographs showing the liked activities, and some of these photographs are scribbled on in ballpoint pen. Certain items are marked with an X ("MAKING THINGS—anything!; PAINTING—on paper, on walls"), and one is crossed out ("HELPING their younger brothers and sisters"), apparently not a universally liked thing.

Lists are concise, declarative, and account-able, but Oberlander's remind us that they are also open-ended, curious, and playful. If listing involves the ordering and categorization of discontinuous, abstracted elements, it also beckons *reorganizing*, *re-sorting*, and *rearranging*. Goody notes how ancient list-making, alongside an inherent pragma-tism, fostered open-ended exploration, "almost for play purposes."[3] With a similar sentiment, lit-erary critic Robert E. Belknap looks beyond a list's apparent efficiency, and instead invites readers to appreciate their non-efficient, "beautifully flawed," and generative potential. "Sometimes we delight in the pattern unwinding before our eyes as its creator sequences the items with a regularity we can keep in step with." Belknap describes the joy of following an author's list, "winding around and through the possibilities."[4]

I experienced a similar creative delight while winding through Cornelia Hahn Oberlander's lists and could not help but reflect on what and how they were teaching me. Of Oberlander's esteemed career, this volume spotlights her undaunted advocacy of play and play spaces, often based on what they *teach*. In the writings collected here, spanning from 1965 to 1984, Oberlander amplifies the pedagogy of play in the modern city. For example, she emphasizes how physical challenges teach cooperation and resilience, how movable parts foster creative rearrangement, and how plants and soil reconnect kids to natu-ral systems. At the same time, adults learn from children at play through research and observation; Oberlander's landscape architecture practice also consulted with children to learn from their own expertise. And perhaps Oberlander's lists *are* a curriculum; they bring her pedagogical arguments to life. Together, the individual pieces encourage discovery, allowing readers to explore and rearrange elements like debris in an Adventure Playground. Her lists are pragmatic but subversive, slipping unexpectedly, edifying joy into an orderly format. This pragmatic subversion radiates from Cornelia Hahn Oberlander's archives: a playground is a plea for utopia, sand specifications advocate for tactile learning, histories of play centre women as catalysts, and the frugal use of discarded materials sparks environmentalist learning.

According to Oberlander, landscape architecture was an ideal profession because while it was challenging and gratifying *work* for the practitioner, it also created spaces of *leisure* and play, for children as well as everyone else. In handwritten notes for a 1975 talk titled "Women and the Idea of Leisure," she advocates for women to join this profession. Women participating in a society-shaping workforce is "the challenge of our time," requiring education, aspiration, confidence, and sacrifice. She offers woman-to-woman mentorship: your career may burden spouses and children, but if you are prepared for a hard path, it is a fulfilling one. She shares specific considerations: do you leave your home to study for a full bachelor's degree of landscape architecture in Guelph, Toronto, Manitoba, or Montreal? Or do you stay at home and train to assist landscape architects

10

drafting, specifying, and supervising construction work? She suggests other job opportunities
available to the landscape architecture–educated
woman: photographer, illustrator, or nature educator. A fulfilling life, Oberlander emphasizes, is more
than just inclusion in the profession; it is multifaceted, one that might include motherhood and
being a spouse, but also must include leisure. "Work
is not every-thing," she writes, "we need free time—
leisure—to nourish our inner impoverishments and
find new strength for the work to be done."[5]

This advice, offered after almost thirty years
of professional experience, echoes Oberlander's
own experiences of migration, of taking space
in a staunchly man-dominated profession, and
of engaging with the intersection of work and life
through an ongoing focus on play-space design.
Oberlander (b. Cornelia Hahn, 1921) grew up
in Mülheim an der Ruhr, Germany, gardening and
immersed in influential ideas that she would bring
forward into her own play designs. Her mother
Beate Hahn, a professional horticulturalist, wrote
books about gardening for and with children,
emphasizing the educational value of caring for
plants. As a teenager, Oberlander made illustrations for her mother's books and was exposed to
thinkers like Friedrich Froebel, proponent of the
kindergarten, whom she continued to reference
later in her career.[6] Oberlander and her family fled
Nazi persecution in Germany in the late 1930s,
and after settling in the northeastern US, she
began her studies at the Cambridge School of
Architecture and Landscape Architecture at Smith
College in 1940. At the time, women were not

allowed at Harvard's Graduate School of Design, but as the Second World War drew away the majority of its students (all men), policies changed and the Department of Landscape Architecture admitted her in a cohort of women students in 1943. The timing was auspicious; Oberlander was already drawn to the modern approach to landscape architecture brewing at the school.[7] She became a key proponent, advocating in school and then in the field for the profession's transformation to match a rapidly changing society.

As Susan Herrington elaborates in her book *Cornelia Hahn Oberlander: Making the Modern Landscape*, Oberlander's career mirrors the story of modern landscape architecture, reflecting the postwar development of the field in North America but also actively pushing and transforming it. Postwar investments in public housing, institutions, and recreational facilities, offered professional landscape architects more opportunities for socially focused public work. Clients of affordable housing and urban parks, in contrast to more traditional upscale residential design, were not affluent, and Oberlander recognized design's responsibility to all.[8] After graduating in 1947, Oberlander worked with landscape architect James Rose before shifting to urban-scale work at the Regional Plan Association of New York. Seeking direct community experience, Oberlander later joined the Citizen's Council on City Planning in Philadelphia as a planner. There, she practised methods of community engagement, using questionnaires and workshops to connect residents with the making of parks and community gardens.[9] Building a reputation as a skilled modern designer, she worked with well-known architects and landscape architects on projects with progressive ideals: from the union headquarters of the United Auto Workers in Detroit, Michigan (with architect Oskar Stonorov), to public housing at Mill Creek (with architect Louis Kahn) and Schuylkill Falls (with Stonorov again), the latter two as an associate with the landscape architect Dan Kiley.[10]

Oberlander applied her community research and engagement skills to the recreational area of 18th and Bigler Streets in Philadelphia, her first solo public project, which opened in 1954. Consulting with community groups, her flexible, rectilinear plan created play areas with some separation between age groups and also shared spaces where kids of different ethnic groups might play together. Sculptural and topographic play elements animated the basic geometry of the plan.[11] The "Turtle Tent" by artist Milton Hebald, one of the sculptures in the playground, was featured in a 1954 brochure of the Play Sculptures Division of Creative Playthings, Inc., emphasizing play sculptures' educational agenda: "to be in harmony with the architecture and philosophy of modern education and the modern community."[12] The 18th and Bigler Streets playground received significant acclaim and laid the groundwork for a career-long engagement with children, education, and play landscapes.

Cornelia Hahn and Peter Oberlander were married in 1953, the same year that she moved to Vancouver. Peter, originally from Vienna, who like his wife had fled Nazi persecution and pursued a degree (in urban planning) at the Harvard Graduate School of Design, had moved to Vancouver in 1950 to establish the University of British Columbia's School of Community and Regional Planning.

In the 1960s and '70s, as Oberlander continued to build her independent practice in a rapidly changing Vancouver, public funding and infrastructure eroded and racially motivated suburban flight by white residents eviscerated urban centres throughout North America. In Canadian cities, plans to clear "blighted," often racialized, neighbourhoods and build mega-highways—new escape routes for the largely white male commuter—loom large. In 1970 Vancouver, Hogan's Alley, an important place of Black culture in the city, was demolished by the Georgia viaduct, and plans for a connected mega-freeway threatened Chinatown.[13] In Toronto, a plan for the Spadina Expressway would run through Chinatown (cancelled in 1971), and large swathes of downtown were cleared for commercial redevelopment and public housing. In Montreal, Little Burgundy residents were displaced for the construction of the Ville-Marie Expressway in the 1970s. And in Halifax, the historic neighbourhood of Africville was demolished by 1970, replaced by infrastructure, and its residents were forcibly relocated.[14] But these plans were met with powerful resistance as communities rejected and, in some cases, overturned them, claiming a right to the city for all—including children. In the writings gathered here, Oberlander does not explicitly discuss the racism and racial politics that underpin these decades, but she recognizes persistent inequalities and stands by the profession's responsibility to support all groups. She warns that a declining birth rate and aging population will mean less capital funding for new construction as well as a need for more multi-use and multi-generational spaces, ones that integrate leisure into the productive areas of the city.[15] The vacant lots she highlights in the 1972 report *Playgrounds ... A Plea for Utopia or the Re-cycled Empty Lot* reflect the environmental injustices that prevailed as freeways barrelled through marginalized communities, and as "nature" became something for those that could afford to leave the city.

Amidst these mega-plans, "man, the planner," Oberlander writes, "has neglected a basic need of his children—the need to play."[16] As Roy Kozlovsky writes, children were prominent in manifestos of modern architecture. In European post–Second World War reconstruction schemes, play spaces were seen as an incremental infill project that could temper the ferocity of slum clearance. Childhood was evoked to critique the Congrès internationaux d'architecture moderne's notion of the Functional City: from images of children playing in Alison and Peter Smithson's 1953 Urban Re-identification Grille, to Aldo van Eyck's influential orphanage and playgrounds. These architects positioned children as victims of the abstract and functionalist modern urban environment.[17] Aldo van Eyck's first Amsterdam playgrounds emerged from sites of violent demolition—the cleared lots of Jewish residents. As Liane Lefaivre accounts, these playgrounds served a redemptive civic role, bringing life to a space of destruction.[18] Like van Eyck, Oberlander saw potential in small vacant lots to address children's need for play, but she also articulated the additional need for plants, insects, and animals; modernist planning disconnected children from soil and water too. A child's need is also a right, and rights must be fought for.

"We have to prod our elected officials daily to remind them of the right of the child for a space for creative play," Oberlander appealed.[19] In "A Short History of Outdoor Play Spaces," she underscores how women led fights that brought public parks acts, parkland appropriation, and supervised playgrounds to Canadian cities in the late nineteenth and early twentieth centuries, overcoming political inertia. She highlights a typical instance when Ottawa's mayor in 1898 agreed to improve the Ottawa Ward Playground, but improbably, at no cost to council: "this again shows us that the local Council of Women had to do most of the work in order to obtain places for children to play."[20] And they did, founding a Playground Association and eventually developing supervised playgrounds. Oberlander centres women's advocacy and leadership, like Miss Ellen Tower and Dr. Marie Zakrezewska, who led the first play gardens in Boston, as well as a Miss Ford who guided Halifax's first playground, writing them into the history of play. A mighty character herself within this lineage, Oberlander continues, "we have to teach parents and we have to teach designers not to think in abstract terms, but in human terms so that our playgrounds will be truly places for play commensurate with the needs of a conserver society."[21] A *conserver society* (advocated for by the Science Council of Canada in the 1970s)[22] opposes the coming ecological catastrophe that *consumer society*, with its fossil fuel addiction and capitalist rulebook, would inevitably bring. In a conserver society designers, engineers, and architects urgently need "to do more with less" and consider the real environmental costs of material consumption despite how bountiful Canada might seem.[23] But in this tumult of urban restructuring, economic scarcity, and ecological threat, Cornelia Hahn Oberlander has characteristically confident plans. The documents gathered here—well accounted in list form— broadcast Oberlander's insistence on play-space design as work of societal and environmental consequence.

"Play is not trivial," Oberlander writes, "educators all over the world stress the significance of early learning and the role of playing in this process."[24] In his influential 1969 book *Design for Play*, architect and playground designer Richard Dattner leans on developmental psychology to inform play-space design: "To put it simply, play is a child's way of learning." Dattner drew from Swiss psychologist Jean Piaget's child development stages (from a toddler's ability for "symbolic play" or make-believe where their needs are met, to a four- to seven-year-old's ability to understand and question rules, to an eight- to twelve-year-old's appetite for group cooperation), to engage those stages in play spaces.[25] Oberlander invoked these age differences in her playground designs, and she contextualized this contemporary research

17

within a long view of educational thinking (including Comenius in the sixteenth century and Froebel's prescient 1826 *Education of Man*).[26] Citing Professor Charles K. Brightbill, she enumerates skills that playgrounds ought to encourage, such as those that "1. help give us a stronger spiritual base, 2. sharpen our abilities to communicate effectively and reflect the social graces, 3. aid body development, movement and motor co-ordination, 4. contribute to safety and survival (e.g. swimming and diving)." Points 5 through 10 include skills that connect us to art, literature, nature, music, drama, and science, and finally, "11. those that encourage us to be of service to others."[27]

In Oberlander's iconic Children's Creative Centre playground at the Canadian Federal Pavilion at Expo '67 in Montreal, these numerous social and physical ambitions are addressed with multifaceted play elements. The Centre's four interior classrooms would offer music, art, and drama to Expo's child visitors, and the designer's task for the playground outside, she wrote, was to interpret the ideas of an educator into a "total environment of 'education for creativity.'"[28] The playground's different areas offered contrasting experiences: contained play for kids under five and their parents, a larger open area rich with interaction, while the covered area aimed at six- to eleven-year-olds offered a quieter zone, including the following elements:

1   Manipulative Wall.
    This is a colourful section of the
    bridge abutment with a series of

Op-Art puzzles which the child can arrange in infinite ways.

2   Musical Screens.
These are four free-standing screens composed of different music instruments, strings, bells, drums, and xylophone. The child can make his own sounds with little wooden felt-covered hammers. The manipulative wall and musical screens are being designed by one of Canada's leading artists, Gordon Smith, of Vancouver.

3   *Story-telling* area with movable bookshelf.

4   Playtables.

5   For those children who like to exercise their muscles on rainy days, a *Commando Net*.[29]

These elements are movable and repositionable, they make sound and art according to the creativity of the child themselves.

The design was not only informed by child studies but it was also the site of study. While children learned in the Children's Creative Centre through play, "leaders in the field of education and recreation" would observe children through a one-way screen, and adults could lean on a rail overlooking the playground from above.[30] Beyond the role of researchers, other adults were critical to a successful playground. Oberlander emphasizes the importance of salaried "play leaders,"

specially trained in pedagogy, to provide guidelines and mediate between older and younger
children. She highlights the first playground
leadership curriculum, offered at McGill University
by Ethel Cartwright in 1912, built on educational
psychology. In a 1906 report, the Playground
Association of America argued that playground
supervisors were essential, playgrounds without
them were "worse than useless."[31] Play leaders
were not meddlers, Oberlander reinforced, they
were a "senior partner." With a gardener's mind-
set, Oberlander references an analogy that play
leaders should carefully *cultivate* play in children,
lest they grow as *weeds*.[32] And in the 1970s,
when declining birthrates and government cuts
meant less work for teachers, Oberlander suggests recommitting to the full-time "playground
leader" as public employment. Successful playgrounds need "a little hardware," she writes,
but "more peopleware."[33]

And not only is play a serious part of a child's
education but it is also their *work*. At a time when
the phrase "women's work" was still used dis-
missively, Oberlander frequently wields the word
"work" when describing the gendered labour
of women or the underappreciated activities of
children on playgrounds. Perhaps she insists that
children "work" to elicit both more political support and respect for the learning taking place?
Appealing to modernist sensibilities, playtime, she
explains, is essential training to be a productive
future worker with a healthy work-leisure balance.[34] Celebrating hard fought union struggles to
achieve the eight-hour workday and the two-day

weekend, she writes that leisure should be appreciated, practised, and something people should be trained in.

Unimpressed with the conventional playground where "a small corner is reserved for rigid and mechanical equipment such as swings, slides, jungle gyms and teeter totters or intimidating concrete monsters,"[35] Oberlander argues that these simply "do not offer enough challenge that today's growing child requires."[36] As a counterpoint, she praises the Adventure Playground movement popularized by the Danish landscape architect Carl Theodor Sørensen and brought to the United Kingdom by Lady Allen of Hurtwood.[37] Lady Allen's 1968 book *Planning for Play* recognized a child's agency, the thrill of calculating risks, and paired these with "tolerant and sympathetic guidance."[38] In the Adventure Playground, creativity is not pre-determined, safety is not guaranteed, and the empty urban lot (that *used* to be suitable for play) is once again legitimized.

Since children are known to make order out of chaos, Oberlander advises handing them chaos—whether a pile of bricks or 2 × 4s—so their creative impulses will "manifest themselves in some sort of 'order.'"[39] In Oberlander's report titled *Playgrounds ... A Plea for Utopia or the Re-cycled Empty Lot*, essential ingredients for an Adventure Playground include the following:

1   left-over lumber ends from construction sites donated regularly by builders in the community

21

2   hammers/saws/nails—choose the best and most suitable in size; have sufficient in number

3   rope

4   old car tires [...]

8   bricks or rocks for building a fireplace for cooking [...]

10 old telephone poles for seats and stepping up-hill [...]

12 appropriate garden tools, seeds, watering cans.[40]

These inexpensive materials and tools are easily found and generate endless possibilities. "When a child is encouraged to construct something on his own, regardless how crude," Oberlander argues, "that object becomes far superior to that child than an identical item which is store bought," challenging mass consumer culture while addressing the scarcity of playground funds.[41] She further suggests a frugal and functional approach to material procurement: bring kids to the dump! "Children like outings to the dump and would bring back very precious finds such as springs, pails, and other treasures," she writes, "These could be used in the playground." Not only would they learn from working with these materials, but they would also learn about recycling and their role within a bigger culture of waste.[42]

In North America, the groundbreaking playgrounds of landscape architect M. Paul Friedberg and architect Richard Dattner facilitated child development research for adults and non-conventional play for children, with experimentation with free movement, risk, and materials, during the same years that Oberlander conceived and built the Creative Children's Centre playground.[43] M. Paul Friedberg and Associates' redesign for the central plaza of the New York City Housing Authority Jacob Riis Houses in Manhattan's Lower East Side (constructed in 1965 and demolished in 2000) offered a playground with stepped and topographic structures that catered to different age groups and physical abilities. Encouraging exploration, agency, and cooperation, Friedberg's design symbolized social participation; press reports, as Mariana Mogilevich writes, viewed Riis residents not as "passive clients of the welfare state, but rather co-creators of their space."[44] Dattner's 1967 West 67th Street Adventure Playground (the name inspired by the earlier-mentioned European precedents) in Central Park was influenced by the sculptor Isamu Noguchi and architect Louis Kahn's 1962 landform-rich playground proposal.[45] It offered stepped landforms, water channels, modular play elements, and was designed to accommodate the playground supervisor. In Canada we can see continuing threads in initiatives from Toronto's junk-forward Adventure Playground on Bathurst Street (1974–1980s), to Evergreen's School Ground Greening program that swapped schoolyard asphalt with mounds and pollinator wildflowers (starting in 2001), to the pop-up adventure playgrounds seen in Montreal today facilitated by the community organization Le Lion et la souris.[46] For Oberlander, the Adventure Playground supported physical risk and creative messiness, and rejected overly prescriptive and sanitized playgrounds. It met limited budgets with cheap and accessible materials, and it valued what was in abundance—vacant lots and children's creativity—as well as what a conserver society would hopefully learn: to do more with less.

If playgrounds are pedagogy, materials are teachers. "The Magic of Sand—Indoors and Out," a lecture on play for children in hospital, is an ode to an ingredient unmatched in economy, flexibility, renewability, and "earthiness." Oberlander details this mundane material of the playground with a great deal of appreciation and understanding. For her, as a playground designer, sand is non-negotiable: "A space to play without sand is a *no-play space*."[47] She animates sand's alchemical nature. With just a little water, it can become different shapes, and with just a little peat and humus, it becomes gardening soil to grow plants in. Sand offers so many opportunities and Oberlander's list includes these:

> You can sift it through your fingers,
>
> You can tip it from your hands,
>
> You can dig in it,
>
> You can eat it,
>
> You can cover yourself with it [...]

You can collect grasses, feathers, sticks, shells, little rocks and you make yourself a garden [...]

You can use it to shape cakes for an imaginary birthday party.[48]

For children in hospital, sand-play—both outdoors and in—is doubly crucial; it can bring learning, fun, and trust-building to the child, and support dexterity from grasping and handling. People will complain, "But what a mess!" But a sandy floor (easily swept!) or the chaos of an Adventure Playground, Oberlander argues again and again, are not the problem; they are precisely the point.

In a list Oberlander titled, "Who can help improve your child's world?" she includes day care services, teachers, major employers, community groups, planning departments, and parents, but Oberlander chose to capitalize one of these agents for emphasis: CHILDREN THEMSELVES.[49] Children know what they want and need, and they should be consulted, and consult them she and her office did. When you ask children what they like to do on an empty lot, Oberlander writes, they are likely to say: "We want mounds to slide down from, we want sand to dig into, we want a tire with a rope hanging from a tree, we want buckets, we want shovels, we want water, we want to plant a garden, and we want to build a tree fort high in the trees." In their responses come inspiration and crucial data. Oberlander the list maker continues, "and so the list will grow, and your enthusiastic clients will give you a list too long to fill."[50] In the Canadian Centre for Architecture's Cornelia Hahn Oberlander fonds, plan-and-detail construction drawings are filed next to children's drawings of playground equipment and vegetables in a garden plot; expert user consultation, submitted in colorful crayon, duly noted.

Whether with hammers and nails, rocking dories, luscious plants, or sand birthday cakes, Cornelia Hahn Oberlander's message about the design of play spaces is loud and clear: make them complex, make them movable, give children agency, and recognize different learning styles, body sizes, and physical abilities. Acknowledging and designing for differences imparts respect for difference; it contests the notion of a "normal" child as well as the design norms that reinforce such a false and problematic idea in the first place. And this reverence for differences perhaps teaches us why Oberlander's lists are so useful to her visions: they offer options with no limit, they campaign, and they propel the joyfully unexpected. In the generous multiplicity of Cornelia Hahn Oberlander's lists, and in the legacy of the play spaces that she designed and built, is a nudge and wink that there are more ways to be, more barriers to overturn, and more adventures to be had.

Notes

1   Jack Goody, *The Domestication of the Savage Mind*
(Cambridge, UK: Cambridge University Press, 1997), 80.

2   Items 1 to 3: "Children Like ...": office-produced list
of children's favourite play and learning activities with photographic illustrations, 1960s, ARCH280011, Cornelia Hahn
Oberlander fonds, CCA. Gift of Cornelia Hahn Oberlander
© CCA; items 4 to 6: a list of points made by Charles K.
Brightbill, presented at Parks and Leisure Seminar, Vancouver,
BC, 26–27 February 1965, quoted in Cornelia Hahn Oberlander,
this volume, 52; items 7 to 9: this volume, 57; items 10 to 12:
this volume, 65; items 13 to 15: this volume, 70.

3   Goody, *The Domestication of the Savage Mind*, 81,
89, 108.

4   Robert E. Belknap, *The List: The Uses and Pleasures
of Cataloguing* (Yale University Press, 2004), xiv, xiii.

5   Cornelia Hahn Oberlander, "Women and the Idea of
Leisure," lecture notes, 1975, AP075.S4.SS3.007, Cornelia
Hahn Oberlander fonds, CCA.

6   Susan Herrington, *Cornelia Hahn Oberlander: Making
the Modern Landscape* (Charlottesville: University of Virginia
Press, 2014), 13–14.

7   Herrington, *Cornelia Hahn Oberlander*, 16, 22–23.

8   Herrington, *Cornelia Hahn Oberlander*, 34.

9   Herrington, *Cornelia Hahn Oberlander*, 40–41.

10   See Herrington, *Cornelia Hahn Oberlander*, 54–56,
for a thorough discussion of Oberlander's early practice.

11   Herrington, *Cornelia Hahn Oberlander*, 52–56.

12   Brochure for play sculptures by Creative Playthings, Inc.,
ca. 1954, recreational area, 18th and Bigler Streets,
Philadelphia, Pennsylvania (1954), 1942–56. 1936–2011,
folder number: 075-014-008, Cornelia Hahn Oberlander
fonds, CCA.

13   See Stephanie Allen, "Fight the Power: Redressing Displacement and Building a Just City for Black Lives in Vancouver" (Master's of Urban Studies Thesis, Simon Fraser University, 2019). Incidentally, around the same time as these plans Oberlander resisted another looming infrastructure, the soon-to-be-iconic monorail of Expo 67, which she did not want to run through and disrupt the Children's Creative Centre playground that she was designing: "I hope, however, it is no longer in the playground." Draft letter from Cornelia Hahn Oberlander to Polly Hill for Children's Creative Centre Playground, Canadian Federal Pavilion, Expo '67, Montreal, Quebec. Ca. 1967, ARCH280447, Cornelia Hahn Oberlander fonds, CCA; another version exists as Letter to Mrs. M.C. [Polly] Hill, 15 September 1965. Library and Archives Canada, Vol 1887 File 4-3-10-5.pdf, p. 8.

14   See Richard Bobier, "Africville: The Test of Urban Renewal and Race in Halifax, Nova Scotia," *Past Imperfect* 4 (1995), 163–80.

15   This volume, 104.

16   Cornelia Hahn Oberlander, "History of Play," 1, c. 1970, AP075.S4.SS1.039, Cornelia Hahn Oberlander fonds, CCA.

17   See Roy Kozlovsky, "Team 10 and Urban Childhood," in *The Architectures of Childhood: Children, Modern Architecture and Reconstruction in Postwar England* (Routledge, 2014), 219–47, and also Juliet Kinchin, Tanya Harrod, Aiden O'Connor, eds., *The Century of the Child: Growing by Design, 1900–2000* (New York: Museum of Modern Art, 2012), 231, 236.

18   Liane Lefaivre, "Space, Place and Play: Or the Interstitial/Cybernetic/Polycentric Urban Model Underlying Aldo van Eyck's Quasi-unknown But, Nevertheless, Myriad Postwar Amsterdam Playgrounds," in *Aldo van Eyck: The Playgrounds and the City*, eds. Liane Lefaivre and Ingeborg de Roode (Amsterdam / Rotterdam: Stedelijk Museum / NAi Publishers, 2002), 45.

19   This volume, 100.

20   This volume, 93.

21   This volume, 100.

22   Geoff Dembicki, "What the 1970s Can Teach Us about Inventing a New Economy," 27 October 2014, https://thetyee.ca/News/2014/10/27/What_1970s_Can_Teach_Us_About_Inventing_New_Economy/, accessed 16 February 2021; and Science Council of Canada, *Canada as a Conserver Society: Resource Uncertainties and the Need for New Technologies* (Ottawa: Supply and Services Canada, 1977).

23   Science Council of Canada, *Canada as a Conserver Society*, 28.

24   This volume, 62.

25   Richard Dattner, *Design for Play* (Cambridge, MA: MIT Press, 1969), 23–31.

26   This volume, 83, 98.

27   Brightbill, quoted in Oberlander, this volume, 53.

28   This volume, 52.

29   Oberlander, "Draft Proposal with Corrections for Children's Creative Centre Playground, Canadian Federal Pavilion, Expo '67, Montréal, Québec," 5. Emphasis and underlining in the original text.

30   This volume, 53; Gabrielle Doiron, "Play on Display: Tracing Encounters with Cornelia Hahn Oberlander's Expo 67 Playground" (Master of Arts Thesis, Department of Art History, Concordia University, 2017).

31   Sara Schmidt, "Domesticating the Parks and Mastering Playgrounds: Sexuality, Power and Place in Montreal, 1870–1930" (Master of Arts Thesis, Department of History, McGill University, 1996), 174.

32   This volume, 90.

33   This volume, 101.

34   Richard Dattner in *Design for Play* emphasized the distinction between work and play, play being a "supremely voluntary undertaking," only in a "condition of freedom," 7.

35   This volume, 62.

36   Oberlander, "History of Play," 2.

37   This volume, 63.

38   Lady Allen of Hurtwood (Marjory Allen), *Planning for Play* (London: Thames and Hudson, 1968), 140.

39   Oberlander, "History of Play," 3.

40   This volume, 65–66.

41   Oberlander, "History of Play," 5.

42   Susan Herrington writes of how Oberlander, dismayed to see the city of Vancouver burning large logs that had washed ashore, convinced the city to instead use them on beaches as seating. Today these grand logs line Vancouver's beaches. Herrington, *Cornelia Hahn Oberlander*, 58.

43   See Clare Cooper, *The Adventure Playground: Creative Play in an Urban Setting and a Potential Focus for Community Involvement* (Working Paper 118, Center for Planning and Development Research, University of California, Berkeley, 1970), 49–59, for discussion of and comparison of European versus North American uptake on the Adventure Playground model.

44   Mariana Mogilevich, "Landscape and Participation in 1960s New York," in *Use Matters: An Alternative History of Architecture*, ed. Kenny Cupers (Taylor and Francis, 2013), 204–6.

45   Alexandra Lange, *The Design of Childhood: How the Material World Shapes Independent Kids* (London: Bloomsbury, 2018), 242, 250.

46   Ed Conroy, "Toronto Once Had the Greatest Playground Ever," *blogTO*, September 2017, accessed 9 June 2021, https://www.blogto.com/city/2017/09/

adventure-playground-toronto-history; "School Ground Greening," Evergreen, https://www.evergreen.ca/our-projects/school-board-collaborations-services/, accessed June 9, 2021; Le Lion et le Souris, accessed 21 December 2021, https://lelionetlasouris.com/.

47   This volume, 69.

48   This volume, 70–71.

49   This volume, 113.

50   This volume, 65.

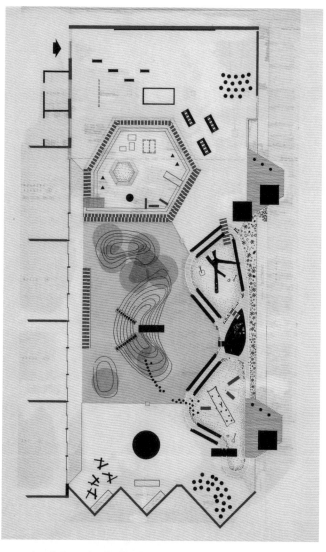

Landscape plan for Children's Creative Centre Playground,
Canadian Federal Pavilion, Expo 67, Montreal, Quebec

Diazotype on paper with ink, graphite, dry transfer and
coloured paper collaged elements, 92 × 88 cm.
Cornelia Hahn Oberlander fonds, CCA Collection. ARCH280457.
Gift of Cornelia Hahn Oberlander

CANADIAN GOVERNMENT PAVI

CHILDREN'S CREATIVE CENTR

Perspective view for Children's Creative Centre Playground,
Canadian Federal Pavilion, Expo 67, Montreal, Quebec

LANDSCAPE ARCHITECT
CORNELIA HAHN OBERLANDER
6029 OLYMPIC ST., VANCOUVER, B.C.

PLAY AREA

Dry transfer on screenprint, 91 × 114 cm.
Cornelia Hahn Oberlander fonds, CCA Collection. ARCH252723.
Gift of Cornelia Hahn Oberlander

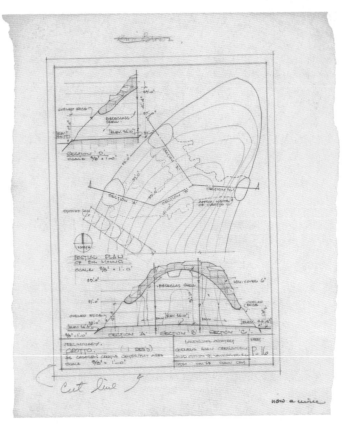

Preliminary plan for grotto and section for big mound for
Children's Creative Centre Playground, Canadian Federal Pavilion,
Expo 67, Montreal, Quebec

Drawing in graphite on translucent paper, 35.4 × 31.43 cm.
Cornelia Hahn Oberlander fonds, CCA Collection. ARCH280453.
Gift of Cornelia Hahn Oberlander

View of treehouse and surrounding area of
Children's Creative Centre Playground, Canadian Federal Pavilion,
Expo 67, Montreal, Quebec

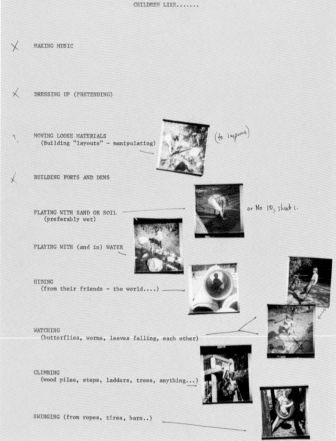

"Children Like …": office-produced list of children's favourite
play and learning activities with photographic illustrations.
Research and reference notes, ca. 1960. Selwyn Pullan Photography.

One of Cornelia Hahn Oberlander's working documents, titled "Children Like …"
and typed on two yellow pages, is a list of twenty-two activities enjoyed
by children—a useful reference for a landscape architecture office designing
playgrounds for them. Next to the listed items are collaged black and white
photographs showing the liked activities, and some of these are scribbled
on in ballpoint pen.

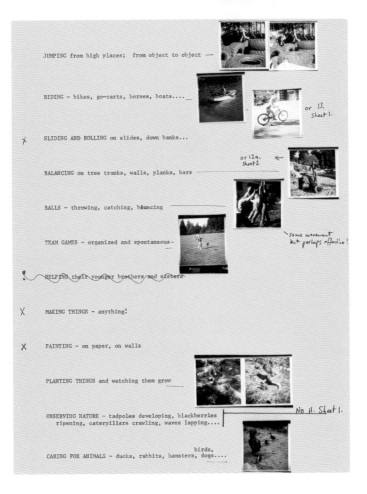

JUMPING from high places; from object to object —

RIDING – bikes, go-carts, horses, boats....

or 13.
Sheet 1.

X   SLIDING AND ROLLING on slides, down banks...

or 12a.
Sheet 2

BALANCING on tree trunks, walls, planks, bars

BALLS – throwing, catching, bouncing

TEAM GAMES – organized and spontaneous~

some movement
but perhaps effective?

HELPING their younger brothers and sisters

X   MAKING THINGS – anything!

X   PAINTING – on paper, on walls

PLANTING THINGS and watching them grow

No 11. Sheet 1.

OBSERVING NATURE – tadpoles developing, blackberries
     ripening, caterpillars crawling, waves lapping....

birds,
CARING FOR ANIMALS – ducks, rabbits, hamsters, dogs....

Typescript and ink on paper with gelatin silver prints, 27.8 × 21.6 cm.
Cornelia Hahn Oberlander fonds, CCA Collection. ARCH280011.
Gift of Cornelia Hahn Oberlander

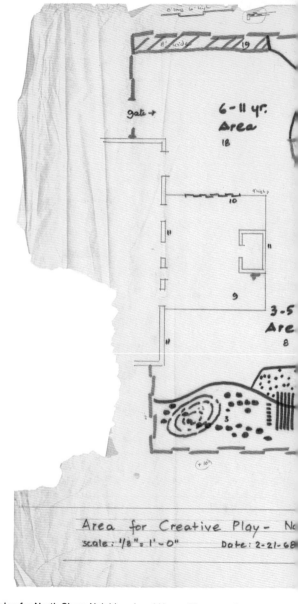

Sketch plan for North Shore Neighbourhood House Playground,
Vancouver, British Columbia, 21 February 1968

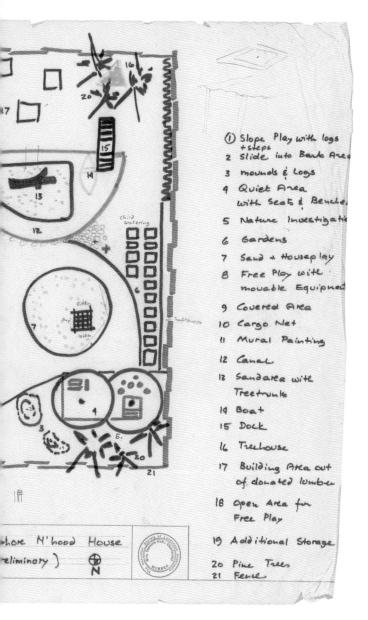

1. Slope Play with logs + steps
2. Slide into Bank Area
3. mounds & Logs
4. Quiet Area with Seats & Benches
5. Nature Investigation
6. Gardens
7. Sand + Houseplay
8. Free Play with movable Equipment
9. Covered Area
10. Cargo Net
11. Mural Painting
12. Canal
13. Sandarea with Treetrunk
14. Boat
15. Dock
16. Treehouse
17. Building Area out of donated lumber
18. Open Area for Free Play
19. Additional Storage
20. Pine Trees
21. Fence

...hore N'hood House
...eliminary)

N

Child Watering

sunflowers

Drawing in ink with graphite on translucent paper, 54 × 62 cm.
Cornelia Hahn Oberlander fonds, CCA Collection. ARCH401910.
Gift of Cornelia Hahn Oberlander

VIEW OF BUILDING AND CANAL AREA

SPACE FOR CREATIVE PLAY

NORTH SHORE NEIGHBOURHOOD HOUSE
225 E 2nd STREET   NORTH VANCOUVER, B.C.

Presentation drawings for North Shore Neighbourhood House Playground, Vancouver, British Columbia, ca. 1968.

Two views showing Space for Creative Play, the building and canal area and the slope and sandbox area.

Whether with hammers and nails, rocking dories, luscious plants, or sand birthday cakes, Cornelia Hahn Oberlander's message about the design of play spaces is loud and clear: make them complex, make them movable, give children agency, and recognize different learning styles, body sizes, and physical abilities.

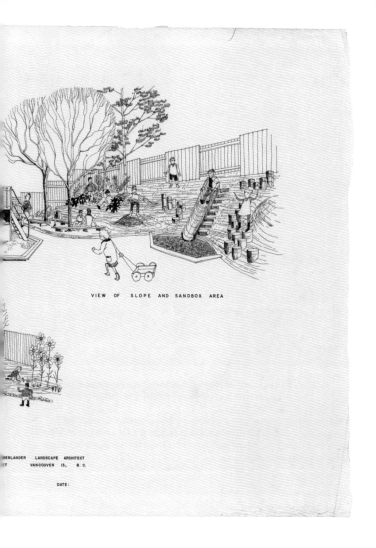

VIEW OF SLOPE AND SANDBOX AREA

BERLANDER   LANDSCAPE ARCHITECT
T   VANCOUVER 13,   B. C.

DATE:

Drawing in ink on translucent paper, 68.5 × 110.5 cm.
Cornelia Hahn Oberlander fonds, CCA Collection. ARCH401912.
Gift of Cornelia Hahn Oberlander

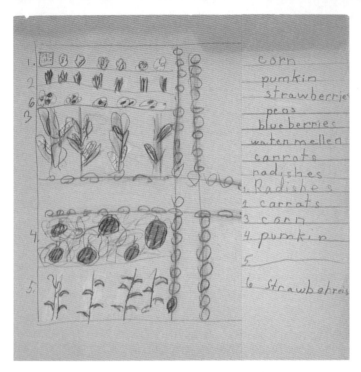

Child's drawing and list for the ideal fruits and vegetables garden.
Research and reference material, c. 1980.

In the Canadian Centre for Architecture's Cornelia Hahn Oberlander
Archives, plan and detail construction drawings are filed next to children's
drawings of playground configurations and vegetables in a garden plot;
colourful feedback noted.

Coloured pencil on paper with graphite, 22.7 × 30.3 cm.
Cornelia Hahn Oberlander fonds, CCA Collection. ARCH283122.
Gift of Cornelia Hahn Oberlander

View of children playing in North Shore Neighbourhood House Playground,
Vancouver, British Columbia

Silver print photograph on cardboard, 25 × 20 cm.
Cornelia Hahn Oberlander fonds, CCA Collection. ARCH401918.
Gift of Cornelia Hahn Oberlander

View of children playing in North Shore Neighbourhood House Playground, Vancouver, British Columbia

Cornelia Hahn Oberlander writes that when you ask children what they like to do on an empty lot, they are likely to say, "We want mounds to slide down from, we want sand to dig into, we want a tire with a rope hanging from a tree, we want buckets, we want shovels, we want water, we want to plant a garden, and we want to build a tree fort high in the trees."

Gelatin chromogenic print, 8.5 × 10 cm.
Cornelia Hahn Oberlander fonds, CCA Collection. ARCH401917.
Gift of Cornelia Hahn Oberlander

Details of play areas, Vancouver, British Columbia, c. 1970.
Selwyn Pullan Photography.
Publication for the Department of Health and Welfare, Canada,
entitled *Playgrounds ... A Plea for Utopia or the Re-Cycled Empty Lot.*

I would like an adventure playground because it would probally give Uan Horne school something to do. The reason why I say this is because I'am always bored. Also we can use it during school. Just think, maybe I will have fun for a change.. I would have lot of fun. I'am sure

Letter of a child to Cornelia Hahn Oberlander
about his or her wishes for a school playground installation

Felt-tip pen on paper, 46 × 30.5 cm sheet.
Cornelia Hahn Oberlander fonds, CCA Collection. ARCH280637.
Gift of Cornelia Hahn Oberlander

A Note on the Texts

Small stylistic changes to correct typographical mistakes or standardize punctuation have been made to the text without being marked. Additions for clarity or for missing words in Cornelia Hahn Oberlander's texts are included in square brackets. Notes that were not from Oberlander's original texts have been preceded by "Editor's Note."

"Spaces for Creative Play in Our Cities," is a draft proposal for Oberlander's Children's Creative Centre Playground, which was constructed as a part of the Canadian Federal Pavilion at Expo '67 in Montreal. The exact date of writing is uncertain, but is most likely between 1965 and 1967. Ca. 1967, ARCH401865, Cornelia Hahn Oberlander Fonds, CCA. Gift of Cornelia Hahn Oberlander © CCA.

Playgrounds … A Plea for Utopia or the Re-Cycled Empty Lot is a report written for the Canadian Minister of National Health and Welfare, and first published by the Department of the Secretary of State in 1972. The text reproduced in this volume is from the second edition of the report, published in 1974 by Recreation Canada, Fitness and Amateur Sport Branch, Department of National Health and Welfare. ARCH280296, Cornelia Hahn Oberlander Fonds, CCA. Gift of Cornelia Hahn Oberlander © CCA.

"The Magic of Sand—Indoors and Out" is a lecture Oberlander delivered to the Symposium on Play for Children in Hospital and in the Community, February 25, 1978. Based on the text's penultimate paragraph, it is likely the symposium took place at the Van Dusen Botanical Gardens in Vancouver. AP075.S3.SS1.164, Cornelia Hahn Oberlander Fonds, CCA. Gift of Cornelia Hahn Oberlander © CCA.

"A Short History of Outdoor Play Spaces" is a talk that Oberlander presented during the International Play Association Congress, Ottawa, Ontario, August 21–26, 1978. AP075.S3.SS1.039, Cornelia Hahn Oberlander Fonds, CCA. Gift of Cornelia Hahn Oberlander © CCA.

The text date and provenance of "Planning for Play Everywhere" is uncertain. However, what appears to be an archival cataloguing note includes a handwritten addition

Spaces for Creative Play
in Our Cities

The capacity to use leisure rightly is
the basis of a man's whole life.
— Aristotle, *Ethics*

Space is at a premium in our urban areas and
time has come for a full assessment of the use of
open spaces. One of the most urgent questions
is, How can we provide in our cities adequate
play spaces for our growing population? Most
cities are overcrowded and man has hardly place
to sit, to walk, to play, or to contemplate at leisure. "Our cities of tomorrow will have to place
man's needs—air, light, and space ahead of those
of the machine, including the automobile."[1]
   We must therefore make our public ser-
vants, our parks boards' members, and our
town planning commissioners aware that their
recreation areas must reflect the needs of
our times. Learning to play cannot be taught
in the home only. It is essential that competent
leaders are available so that children of each
neighbourhood learn to use the resources fully
that their city provides. All over the world today
educators, playground designers, and directors
of parks talk about the necessity of learning
to play at an early age.
   Playgrounds must therefore encourage
absorption in activity and unselfconscious

concentration. They ought to provide seclusion from disturbing or diverting influences, afford an exit from the everyday pressures, and give to the child at play the possibility of a make-believe world.

Professor Brightbill at a recent Vancouver seminar suggested that leisure time ought to be time for self-fulfillment and not time of just being amused or entertained by gadgets. We must therefore instill in the very young interests and skills to prepare them for the new opportunities for leisure. According to Professor Brightbill, we ought to encourage skills that:

1   help give us a stronger spiritual base

2   sharpen our abilities to communicate effectively and reflect the social graces

3   aid body development, movement, and motor co-ordination

4   contribute to safety and survival (e.g. swimming and diving)

5   make use of the creative hands as in the graphic and plastic arts

6   take us deep into literature

7   bring us close to nature, and especially outdoor living

8   create music, or at least make it possible for us to enjoy it

9   provide the opportunity to express ourselves through drama in a variety of forms

10   open the door of the scientific world and

11   those that encourage us to be of service to others.

Into this setting then the Children's Creative Centre, a part of the Canadian Federal Pavilion at Expo '67 in Montreal, has been conceived. The Centre consists of four classrooms where the best methods in music, art, drama, and nursery education will be taught. The project director is the well-known educator, Mrs. H.P. Hill of Ottawa.[2] The Centre will draw its children from the families visiting the Canadian Pavilion. It is estimated that about 75,000 youngsters will pass through the Centre during the six months of the World's Fair. This area will not only serve children, but also leaders in the field of education and recreation who will be able to observe through a one-way screen all activities. Instruction will be provided by professionally trained specialists. The children will have a stimulating experience combined with fun and will be exposed to new ideas which may spark an interest in their future.

The Playground is the outdoor waiting room for the Children's Creative Centre. In size it can be compared to a city "vest-pocket park"—60' × 120' in the open area and 60' × 40' in the covered area.

Upon being invited to design this area, I asked myself, What is it that children really like to do? They like to run, they like to climb, to crawl, to build, to feel contrasting textures and see colours. In creating this playground it was the designer's task to interpret the ideas of an educator and to relate those to design principles in order to achieve a total environment of "education for creativity," as Mrs. Hill calls it.[3]

The restful garden—like [the] atmosphere of gentle mounds, pine trees, and hedges—is purposefully created to contrast with the concrete and asphalt jungle effect of the world of the city child.

There are three parts:

I	Covered area	6- to 11-
II	Open area	year olds
III	Nursery area	3- to 5-year-olds

Covered Area
This is designed for quiet play and contains:

1. Manipulative Wall. This is a colourful section of the bridge abutment with a series of Op-Art puzzles which the child can arrange in infinite ways.

2. Musical Screens. These are four free-standing screens composed of different music instruments, strings, bells, drums, and xylophone. The child can make his own sounds with

little wooden felt-covered hammers. The manipulative wall and musical screens are being designed by one of Canada's leading artists, Gordon Smith,[4] of Vancouver.

3 *Story-telling area* with movable bookshelf.

4 <u>Playtables</u>.

5 For those children who like to exercise their muscles on rainy days, a *Commando Net*.

Open Area

1 *Viewing Platforms or docks.*
The Docks extend over the present waterway. This area is meant for children to relax and quietly watch boats pass by.

2 *Sand and Canal Area.* To reach the sand area, one can balance on logs or cross tiny, arched bridges or just leap. A 16" wide, 4" deep canal winds around the sand areas, with flowing water. Boats can be assembled and floated, or children can actually pan for "gold" as the top layer of the canal bed is to have polished agate and fool's gold. There is an old "Dory" from Nova Scotia which rocks to the motion of the children's imaginary storms—or lulling calm.

3   Well scaled sand toys are available
    for digging.

4   The upper sand area contains a
    large barkless tree lying on its side for
    climbing and on the lower area is
    a hollow stave pipe with peep holes,
    to crawl through.

5   A planting area near the fence of
    bullrushes relieves the monotony
    of the fence.

6   Moving to the bottom of the plan,
    a blackboard on the wall for drawing
    or school play is installed. The other
    nooks have store and house play areas
    and in one of them are actual "Pan
    Abode" logs with specially loose-
    fitting joints for easy construction
    of play houses.

7   The circle in front of the store play
    nook is a "Wobble-Walk," 10' in
    diameter; children will try to get
    across it and sink and tumble, like
    walking on an immense feather bed.

8   <u>Tree-House Area</u>. In order to give
    some undulation to the ground, three
    small hillocks with pine trees are
    placed in the position shown on the
    plan. These are to provide a natural
    feeling to the area and also act as
    a visual and noise barrier for the
    children in the classroom. The highest

mound is 8' high and has a steep wooden chute from the top. It can be reached by cedar steps. The trees in the mound area are large white pines. The mounds will be sodded with a grass selected for intensive use.

9   The main mound has a secret tunnel built into it through which children can crawl.

Nursery Area is separated by a 4' high cedar hedge. It contains:

1   Sand box

2   Water-play area

3   Rabbit cages

4   Rocking boat

5   Hollow blocks

6   Play house

7   Climbing tepee

8   Flower pots with a great variety of plants are placed on the periphery to be watered and studied by the children.

9   Step-seating arrangement has been made for mothers to sit with shy youngsters and help them overcome any fear of strangeness.

This playground, though specially designed for Expo '67, ought to provide some new ideas for our crowded urban communities. Everywhere there are areas that could be made into vest-pocket parks with mounds, ravines, tree houses, streams for wading, and places for building. After all, the "Adventure Playgrounds" of Great Britain and Denmark stimulate most the child's imagination.

Whatever we do, let us build playgrounds that will help the young to develop a feeling of self-fulfillment in the "Age of Leisure" and make recreation a creative experience.

Notes

1   Professor Charles K. Brightbill, Professor and Head of Department of Recreation and Municipal Park Administration, University of Illinois, during the Parks and Leisure Seminar, February 26 to 27, 1965, University of British Columbia.

2   Editor's note: Polly Hill (1917–2015), early childhood development educator, author, film maker, and community organizer.

3   Editor's note: see Polly Hill, "Children's Creative Centre at Canada's Expo '67," *Young Children* 22, no. 5 (May 1967): 258.

4   Editor's note: Gordon A. Smith (1919–2020), British-born, Vancouver-based modernist painter.

Playgrounds ... A Plea for Utopia or the Re-Cycled Empty Lot

The spirit of play is vital to all humanity, the basis of most of the happiness of mankind, the means by which humanity advances creatively, scientifically, intellectually, and socially. Not only is it vital to childhood but the spirit of play is vital to all mankind. In understanding children's play, we will have understood the key to the processes which educate the whole child. Because we live in a highly civilized world, all play activities need the kindly, sympathetic, understanding teacher who will provide materials, suggestions, kindliness, freedom, and space, and who, by example, will set standards of behaviour and discipline with which children can experiment creatively to their own advantage.[1]
— Neville V. Scarfe, dean of education, University of British Columbia

The concept of play is illustrated by the cover sketch [see page 42]. Children love to be where the action is; they make no hard and fast distinction between work and play. Adults, however, often misunderstand the child's urge to play; we forget in our crowded urban life to provide spaces for them to play by building, digging, or moving things around and manipulating these at their will. Play is not trivial; educators all over the world stress the significance of early learning and the role of playing in this process.

It has been demonstrated that much fundamental learning takes place before the age of five and therefore we must build community playgrounds that relate to this insight.

As we drive through towns and cities we admire well-treed and well-manicured grass areas in most public parks. Usually a small corner is reserved for rigid and mechanical equipment such as swings, slides, jungle gyms, and teeter totters or intimidating concrete monsters. These sorts of playgrounds have only occasional or intermittent customers, for short-term visits and therefore fail to meet the educator's goal. The essential ingredients for playgrounds are space and a good variety of items that can be manipulated in an infinite number of ways so as to elicit new responses from the child as he plays. Physical activity such as derived from climbing on a jungle gym is not enough if the child is to find self-fulfillment in play; psychological as well as kinetic stimulation are needed for self-development. So far this has been done most successfully through the design of Adventure Playgrounds.

The Adventure Playground

Lady Allen of Hurtwood, an early advocate of the Adventure Playground in England writes in her most recent book, *Planning for Play*: "Adventure playgrounds are places where children of all ages can develop their own ideas of play. Most young people, at one time or another, have a deep urge to experiment with earth, fire, water and timber, to work with real tools without fear of undue criticism or censure. In these playgrounds their love of freedom to take calculated risks is recognized and can be enjoyed under tolerant and sympathetic guidance."[2]

The Adventure Playground was invented in Denmark during the German occupation when the "Emdrup Junk Playground" was opened in 1943. A well-known landscape architect, Professor C. Th. Sørensen,[3] had designed many formal playgrounds in Copenhagen, but was impressed by the fact that children seemed to prefer messing about in junk yards and building sites, and developing their own brand of play with waste objects which they found there.

With great perception and courage, he started the "Emdrup Junk Playground" in a housing estate outside Copenhagen. He and the children were fortunate in its first understanding leader, John Bertelsen, who was a trained nursery-school teacher and an ex-seaman; he was well-equipped to tackle an experiment in learning and teaching. Emdrup gave the world a new concept of play and is still influencing playground design 31 years later.

So far the idea of the Adventure Playground has found little acceptance in North America and we have only spotty and temporary examples in Canada. The Adventure Playground is really the old empty lot that many children of earlier generations took for granted in most Canadian communities. Let's find and re-create these occasional informal spaces and thereby recycle the empty lot as a conscious effort to achieve creative play spaces. This can best be done through the children themselves but guided by trained leadership and supported by the parent.

The Site   The site may be one or two city lots. It should be in public ownership with well-drained loamy soil; it should have a few trees for shade and be close to the homes of the children it is designed to serve. It should be made into an area separated from the diverting and disturbing influences of our present-day, car-oriented world. It should give the child the possibility to play in his make-believe world and discover his own innate skills in the presence of a well-trained unobtrusive leader.

The Leader   A competent leader is the key to the successful playground. He has to be a resourceful person with infinite patience and one who can develop human trust amongst the children and the neighbourhood. From then on, the Adventure Playground will build itself.

Think of yourself aged ten or maybe twelve, what did you like to do on the empty lot? When you ask today's children, you will hear pretty much the same; they are likely to say: "We want mounds to slide down from, we want sand to dig into, we want a tire with a rope hanging from a tree, we want buckets, we want shovels, we want water, we want to plant a garden, and we want to build a tree fort high in the trees." And so the list will grow and your enthusiastic clients will give you a list too long to fill and so you start involving the parents; hopefully they will help to realize some of the wishes and aspirations of the children and the community; thus making it an ongoing adventurous process.

The essential ingredients for an Adventure Playground are:

Suggested Materials

1   left-over lumber ends from construction sites donated regularly by builders in the community

2   hammers | choose the best
        saws | and most suitable in size;
        nails | have sufficient in number

3   rope

4   old car tires

5   pulleys

6   wooden boxes

7   cardboard cartons

8   bricks or rocks for building a fireplace for cooking

9   pipe ends and wire mesh, plastic pipe
10   old telephone poles for seats and
     stepping uphill
11   gardening earth
12   appropriate gardening tools, seeds,
     watering cans
13   sandbox area 18" deep, filled with
     cement mixing sand; excess excavation
     will make a mound. The sandbox
     should have buckets and shovels, etc.
     A watering hose should be connected
     to a hose bib.
14   carpenter's bench
15   storage shelter and "Magic Box."

The illustrations [see pages 45 to 47, this volume]
may give an idea how these materials are used.

Experience has shown that the best
Adventure Playgrounds are simple and flexible
with a lot of unfinished space and full of
variety and surprises; the "Magic Box" which
can be stored in the shelter should contain new
items which keep the children fascinated, especially the younger ones aged three to eight who
undoubtedly will come to visit. Their interests
can be satisfied and diverted without getting in
the way of the "older builders."

The overall programme can be supplemented
with inexpensive equipment. Such material
can be found in our city dumps, beaches, river
edges, etc. Children like outings to the dump
and would bring back very precious finds
such as springs, pails, and other treasures.
These could be used in the playground. Other

important ideas for the playground would be a garden using either small beds 3' × 3' square for each child or one large area for all, depending on the ages and interests of the children.

The total programme will be one that encourages children to play in larger and smaller groups, communicate with one another, cooperate, and share. The building of their structures will help them to develop motor skills, coordination, and self-confidence.

An Adventure Playground, if successfully run during a summer, ought to pave the way for more permanent institutions of its kind and encourage community programs of this nature all year-round. It should guide today's children into becoming self-motivated, confident, and creative adults.

Creative play in an informal setting will make the playground the adventure in learning that the empty lot provided unselfconsciously for earlier generations.

Notes

1   Editor's note: N.V. Scarfe, "Understanding Children's Play," in World Organisation for Childhood Education, *Report of the 8th World Assembly* (Zagreb, Yugoslavia, July 31 to August 6, 1960), 34.

2   Editor's note: Lady Allen of Hurtwood (Marjorie Allen), *Planning for Play* (London: Thames and Hudson, 1968), 55.

3   Editor's note: Carl Theodor Sørensen (1893–1979).

The Magic of Sand—
Indoors and Out

The basic elements of the Ancients were: *earth,
water, fire,* and *air.* This may explain the yearning in every child to play with water and sand
in the fresh air, and sometimes light a fire. A
space to play without sand is a *no-play space.*
Sand has magic and magnetic qualities to which
all children gravitate. It has been so through
the ages. Pictures by the Dutch painter, Pieter
Bruegel,[1] show us games on sandy soil in the
town square and innumerable references occur
in literature. A young Swiss gentleman, for
example, wrote in the year of 1550: "Wherever
I could find a little bit of sand, or earth on the
streets, I started to dig holes, and with found
stones I built castles and towers. I loved to mix
lime and clay, and not even hard and frequent
spankings could discourage me from this activity which I enjoy to the present day."[2]

As one travels through the world, whether
it be here or abroad, you find children most
happily at play on a pile of sand; while the
parents work in the fields, or the mother sits
chatting with a friend on a bench under a tree.
The sand area is the place where the most
absorbing play takes place. Play for the child
is work, a kind of research and adventure
which should be an enjoyable experience from
which the child returns fully satisfied, joyous,

and gay. Sand areas represent the most flexible play, renewable, inexpensive, and "earthy" play material. Today, with increased costs, natural materials should be used wherever possible. At the present time we are too conscious of hygiene to use this basic material more frequently. With this attitude we are depriving all our children from a play-learn experience and not making it ready for the work-leisure cycle ahead.

Søren Kierkegaard, the famous Danish philosopher of the nineteenth century, observed: "you learn to know a child by observing it in play."[3] Have you ever observed children at the beach? Why not make miniature play situations indoors or outdoors possible? Sand has qualities that no other material can muster. It has:

> texture
> colour
> pliability.

What can you do with it?

> You can sift it through your fingers,
> You can tip it from your hands,
> You can dig in it,
> You can eat it,
> You can cover yourself with it,
> You can make imprints of your feet,
>   your legs, your hands,
> You can collect grasses, feathers, sticks,
>   shells, little rocks and you make
>   yourself a garden or you can,

Take empty tins or ice-cream containers
    and wooden spoons to the beach, or
You can strain the sand with an old
    colander,
You can fill old cooking pots, or funnel it
    into plastic bottles or you can shovel it
    into paper cartons,
You can load it onto trucks, pull it around
    in carts and wheelbarrows,
You can weigh it,
You can build roads and tracks for Dinky
    Toys and,
You can use it to shape cakes for an
    imaginary birthday party,
You can smooth it out and draw in it with
    your fingers or sticks,
You can make sand castles and buildings.

Now these are just a few things you can do with
sand. It is endless in its shapes and its texture
is appealing. In combination with water, sand
takes on different shapes. You can make yourself
a little lake on which you can float paper boats
or pieces of wood—you may jump into it—you
paddle in the pool—you make mud pies with
water, you water your garden, and if you can
visualize that all these wonderful play experiences can be had with just two ingredients,
namely sand and water, it certainly should be
mandatory that all playgrounds are designed for
sand play, indoors as well as outdoors.

For indoors a finer sand is used, and there
are several ways of making sand-play possible.
Indoors:

71

A sunny playroom with plants should be used, where a box filled with sand sits on a table with or without castors. The box should be 57 centimetres by 72 centimetres by 7 centimetres. The playroom should have shelves holding boxes with toys so that the child may choose whatever it wants to play with or act out.

However, in the hospital setting one should ameliorate the impact of the environment on the child. Sand-play could help to relieve this impact and allow the child to play for fun, for learning. It is this type of play which will help develop the person and give this child a feeling of trust of the outer world. It will encourage dexterity amongst the handicapped—grasping, visualizing, discovering. The sand tables should be in a playroom with shelves filled with colourful tiles, clay, old and new toys, wooden toys, trees, houses, blocks, so that it will make a rich environment in which the child can play. Water should be readily available, maybe in the form of a watering can or a miniature hose connected to a sink. For some patients a sand box on wheels may be the answer and for some, a sand box in a covered area.

Mutterings will be heard "But what a mess!" These pictures will show you that this does not need to be so. [If] a table with four legs, or [a] box placed on a table with four legs with a wide margin around it, and a suitable cover be used, it will not be a mess. In hospital settings, a whole room can be filled with pliable sand and a wooden floor around it, so that the child is exposed to a complete play environment.

For the out of doors, the sand area should be large enough for everyone to claim a territorial space. That is 10 to 25 square metres per child, which is 30 to 75 square feet per child, which means for 10 children a sand area of 300 square feet (or 15' × 20') is necessary. The sand area should be located in a secluded, wind-free, sunny spot, with some trees for shade and seclusion. It must be at least 3' deep to allow for digging large holes and lined with rock to drain the water away. Sand used for outdoors is a coarser sand that falls readily off the clothes. There should be a ramp for access, for the handicapped, with seats around for play leaders or parents, or it could be bordered with stones or wood. Then there is a space for creative and experimental play. Children love to create things, and the first step is always finding out about the materials and how to use them. The child who experiments with a new material or medium often finds he has something new and exciting, and here the versatility of sand is unsurpassable. There are examples of sand play with platforms built into the sand box which are helpful. It is wise to locate play areas at the hospital so that these may also be used by children in the community. It makes for a friendlier atmosphere all round.

And last but not least, these is one more form of sand—the soil—if we add to it peat and humus, we have good gardening soil. This leads me to another aspect, namely the magic of growing things. In hospital settings, as well as in nursery schools, or on play areas near our homes, there should be places where the children will watch beans, peas, or nasturtiums grow, or anything else they would like to plant. To give gardening lessons to children is the most exciting of tasks—luckily here at the Van Dusen Botanical Gardens in Vancouver, a young lady on the staff would be delighted to come with her kit of tricks to show how one can garden with children in schools or hospitals.

Conclusion

The international year of the child will be celebrated in 1979; why don't we look at our communities and see how we can find inexpensive places for playing and learning?

Notes

1   Editor's note: Pieter Bruegel, the Elder (c. 1525–30 to 1569). See, for example, his 1560 painting, *Children's Games*.

2   Editor's note: This appears to be a reference to Andreas Ryff (1550–1603), a merchant, politician, and historian, whose autobiographical writings record his life until 1574. See also this volume, 105n2.

3   Editor's note: Attribution uncertain, but the same text is quoted in Lady Allen of Hurtwood (Marjory Allen), *Space for Play: The Youngest Children* (World Organisation for Early Childhood Education, 1964), 7.

A Short History of Outdoor Play Spaces

Play in Human Settlements is the theme of this conference. Play in human settlements is both an *old* idea and a *very* new one.

OLD

to live in organized settlements meant to be a *pleasure* where there were *deliberate* places and spaces for recreation and play in a socially accepted fashion, e.g. at the Agora in Greek towns or the market or City Hall square of the medieval town. Because play was the privilege of the few and the rich—historically a minute number of people were only able to play. Vast majority had to work or slave from dawn to dusk 6½ or 7 days without holidays.

NEW

In the struggle for survival there was no place or time for play. Therefore time and places for play in settlements for *ALL*— young and old—rich and poor, in short for everyone, that is the inheritance of social revolutions in the late nineteenth and early twentieth centuries.

In the next few days, we shall think how we can rearrange our cities to incorporate the fabric of play and make it possible for everybody to enjoy himself, especially the small child. The United Nations' Declaration of the Rights of the Child states: "the child shall have full opportunity for play and recreation … society and the public authorities shall endeavour to promote the enjoyment of the right."[1] This is a global wish and for centuries we have tried to achieve this.

Let us regress in time and ask ourselves:

1   Where and how did our children play?

2   Who formulated ideas for play?

3   How can we insure and improve the child's right to play in the future?

Maybe a short historical vignette will help, since our inheritance from the past should guide us in the future. Johan Huizinga, in his most profound book *Homo Ludens*, a study of play elements in society, wrote in 1938 that "play has left a timeless imprint on world civilization and world culture." Here we shall briefly look into the history of mankind as it relates to play through the ages, with special emphasis on outdoor play in our cities in the nineteenth and early twentieth centuries. Leisure, or time away from work, was not known in the early days of our civilization when agriculture was the basis of livelihood. Leisure and work were intertwined and insepa-rable; this work/play cycle regenerated the spirit and readied the person from zero to eighty for the next step. This is illustrated in an Egyptian relief in which a variety of past times and sports are depicted, including hunting in the desert, or spearing fish from the river. Noblemen enjoyed themselves in the garden, surrounded by family and friends. The peasants indulged in wrestling matches and the soldiers performed war dances while other members of the population performed dances for religious rites, or indulged in ball games. The Ancient Hebrews performed dances, though mostly religious, such as at funerals or harvest festivals; one of the earliest forms of recreation of these ancient people was swimming. The Talmud commands the father of the ancient Hebrews to teach his sons a trade and swimming; in fact swimming became such a popular pastime that it was forbidden on the Sabbath. This is one of the earliest references to the work/play cycle. Swimming was also practised by the Assyrians and Persians. In Persia, boys at the age of seven were trained in running contests, while girls were trained in domestic arts, such as singing and listening to storytellers. Wealthy Egyptian parents allowed the child much leisure time; they were given elaborate and beautiful toys to play with, such as covered balls and dolls with moveable limbs; they played chess and senet, tug-of-war, and many other games. In those days recreation and play took place anywhere. One swam in the lake, or the ocean, one danced and saw performances or other spectator sports in the city squares or at the Temple, or hunted in the woods and fields. In the homes of the rich, professional magicians, storytellers, and jugglers amused the families and friends.

The culture of cities occurred in the *classical period*. It was a time of great concern for beauty in buildings, respect for truth, and emphasis on the cult of a sound mind and sound body to produce the whole man. The Greeks were the first to realize the importance of play; Plato in his book, *The Laws*, urged that children ought to be allowed to play freely, and went so far as to propose the setting up of nursery schools, where gymnastics, music, and dancing were taught to the very young, as it was deemed good for body and soul, under guidance of nurses who were to have an eye on the children's behaviour. In short then, play was accepted as part of life. Books and drawings of the time tell us of the many games played by these children. They are very much the same games that our children still play today. There were rattles, balls, rocking horses, little carts, cups and saucers for their dolls' dinner parties, small gardening tools, knuckle bones for games of skill, and many other games which we still know today.

Some of these ideas of Plato's teaching were incorporated in the nineteenth century by Friedrich Froebel who set up the first kindergarten. In Rome between 106 and 140 BC, Cicero regarded education as a process by which Man can perfect himself. He recognized the importance of early learning, so much so that we inherited from him learning by rote. This, of course, was entirely designed for boys, the carriers of Roman culture. Roman society was highly structured and the lifecycle of the nobleman contrasted vividly with the squalor of the poor or the slave. The young girl was encouraged to play with dolls, stilts, tops, running, jumping, swimming, riding, and martial arts; they were often taken to spectator sports by their families. Games took place in stadiums, social halls, open theatres, public parks, and the forum, the public library, in private gardens, near temples, and other public buildings. It was, after all, the Greek and Roman civilization that gave us the city as an art form, and in it, the citizens contributed to the sciences, the arts and literature, and achieved the leisure to play. Philosophy flourished and Man became civilized.

In the Middle Ages, the cities became fortresses walled for protection. Man had little space for himself. The town was a work of art—but crowded. Everything centred around the Cathedral and the City Hall; recreation and play occurred in front of them, like the famous horseraces in Siena, and usually as part of the church ritual. However, children could play everywhere. The city as living experience had more effect on the training of the young than the formal school. Children went with their parents to the fields to seed and harvest or else watch a troop of jugglers perform in the city square. In the medieval period, the family structure was a strong one in which the father ruled with an iron hand and he was the undisputed authority. Much of the life of these medieval people centred around the guild and the trade which they pursued. The craft guild put on mystery plays and fairs that moved from town to town throughout the seasons. The guild system passed on to us the respect for every man's trade and we have learned that the worker has as much latent sensibility as any other human being. It was after all the stonemasons that gave us the beautiful cathedrals and their sculptures. The illuminators and painters were scribes that gave us religious books and it is since this era that we realize that the daily education of the senses, as experienced in the medieval town, is the elemental groundwork of all forms of higher education. When it permeates our daily life, the community may spare itself the need of arranging courses in art appreciation.

There are but a few records of how children played in the past; none is better than the magnificent painting of the Dutch painter, Pieter Bruegel, of *Children's Games* (1560), showing all the many games that were played at his time in Holland. We see an open space, parents buying bread, parents sweeping and the children playing. It depicts a city which included children and there are few grown-ups in the picture. Many of the games are those which we still see today, such as tops, windmills, masks, piggy back, blind man's buff, headstands, horses, climbing, wading, and the little girls have a pretend wedding and a whole doll's house at their disposal. We see children swinging, digging in the sand, riding hobby horses, playing with drums and whistles, walking on stilts, wrestling, and enjoying themselves in general. Through this magnificent genre of painting we get an idea of what life was like for a child.

Most children yearned for places to play. In 1550 the autobiography of a young Swiss nobleman in Basel, Andreas Ryff, tells us of his yearnings for play: "Whenever I found a little heap of sand or a bit of earth in the lanes, I dug big holes and I gathered stones, building towers, houses and walls; I also enjoyed very much to play around with lime, water and earth, and often after that I got very hard spankings; but nobody could rob me of this pleasure of building which I still love to this very day."[2] Though hard and frequent spankings were a given, sand play already then was the best form of play. It shows the eternal yearning of a child to play with dirt—only 300 years later this basic need became recognized, as we shall see.

During the Renaissance the Court declined, and many people, especially the nobility, tried to escape the chaos and crowded conditions to settle on their country estates such as Versailles and Vaux le Vicomte. The lower urban classes were left in the crowded city without time for leisure, while the middle-class craftsmen and artisans usually spent what leisure time they had in drinking and carousing, while the clergy emphasized that learning was a most worthwhile activity. Therefore, it was not unusual to hear that John Amos Comenius (1592–1672), a monk of the Order of the Bohemian Brothers, published the first book for children, called the *Orbis Pictus*. Published in 1658, this book gives us an excellent idea of what children were exposed to regarding their knowledge of nature, science, trades, soldiering, baking, shipbuilding, and woodworking, explaining each item in detail. The chapter on social games and children's play defines Play: "As soon as the human soul begins to reflect, it begins to employ itself," which is a good insight into the play process. Each item is described in English, German, French, and Latin, demonstrating emphasis on learning languages at a young age, to expanding the horizon of the child. Comenius became so famous that in 1641 the English invited him to reform their school system according to his principles. Later he travelled to Sweden where he set up systems of educational institutions consisting of a maternal school, a vernacular school, a Latin school, and academy. The maternal school was under the direction of the mother, and can be compared with the seventeenth-century École Maternelle in France. The mother attended to the physical welfare of her child and offered him opportunities for cheerful play. Comenius outlined exercises for children to teach them to think and speak. He encouraged the play interests of children by using objects, pictures, and puzzles in the younger schools. He in fact worked for universal systems of education, which included equal opportunities for women.

During the seventeenth century, attempts were made in cities to build parks and to convert city streets at festival time into dance and play places with brightly coloured banners and music. Open spaces and pleasure parks on converted city fortifications, like the Tuileries

Garden in Paris, became places for the rich to be seen and to enjoy themselves.

The outlook for public recreation remained dim for the poor. No land was acquired by any city for this. Life in seventeenth- and eighteenth-century Paris was dreadful; children of the rich were sent to the country and separated from their families because the pollution, the stench, the filth of the city made it too unhealthy for them. This eventually led to Rousseau's book *Emile* (equality, fraternity, and co-op).

At the same time, in contrast to the lavish life of the nobility in Europe, the early settlers brought to America their Puritan ideals to sustain them in a hostile environment. Self-reliance and frugality were stressed, play was sinful and against prevailing religious practices because it implied idleness. Industry and thrift were encouraged. This outlook on life had far reaching effects on our own attitudes towards cities in North America till today. We are still suffering from these puritanical ideals and that is why it is so difficult for urban designers to introduce "pleasure areas" into our cities. It was not until 1963 that we had Sunday movies in Vancouver, for instance; and that life in the city should be a pleasure and include dancing and music in public in city squares only happened yesterday. The main recreation in Colonial America was visiting neighbours and doing things together such as snow plough-ing, seeding, and harvesting. Group work was common practice for all tasks which would better be accomplished with another person helping, like making soap, apple butter, hooking rugs, or the loading of logs. Neighbour would join neighbour in accomplishing chores and after a few days, the favour would be returned. In addition to repaying the work by doing the same or similar work, the helping neighbour would be rewarded with Jamaica rum, or hard cider. Dinner recipes were exchanged between neighbours to vary dull menus. Common religious practices played a central community role. Praying with and for, as well as visiting the sick, became not only a friendly gesture but an important social function. It gave people a chance to exchange news and gossip and provided a break in the hard, everyday routine of pioneer life. The main characteristic of past times in Colonial America was doing things together like knitting bees, quilting bees, ploughing bees, and husking bees. These were all related to making a living and surviving in a harsh environment, yet had social and recreational meaning too. This sharing was an attitude which we should not forget. In Colonial times only the very young children had any play time. The moment the child reached the age of twelve, he or she had to help make a living. There were not many things to play with except homemade bows and arrows, willow whistles, tops, marbles, ribbons, and paper. They were simple toys and evenings were spent in making valentines, dressing dolls, or cutting out. May Day celebrations were important; mainly, the child watched the adults or partook in their work.

The first reference to the right to play is probably contained in a letter of the nine-year-old John Quincy Adams (1767–1848), eldest son of the second president of the United States. John Quincy's father was serving in the Continental Congress at the time and the young boy had to stay at the family farm in Braintree, Massachusetts, helping his mother to manage the farm. He writes in 1777: "It is much nicer to receive letters than to write them. I am a very sad figure when it comes to writing essays. Everything goes around in my head. My thoughts are directed to looking for birds' eggs and playing with all sorts of little things that I even get angry at myself sometimes. Mama has a very difficult task to try and teach me things and keep me with the books, and I admit that I am very much ashamed of myself. And now I have come to grips with myself that I shall be more eager to learn in the next few weeks. I have set a goal that I shall read the Third Volume of Rollins History or at least half of it, and I hope that I shall keep to his goal and then I shall have better things to tell you. I would like, dear sir, that you will set down rules so that I can divide my learning time and my play time properly."[3] This letter is most likely one of the first aspirations of a child to the right to play and not an unusual wish.

Life in New England centred around the commons. There were no special places set aside for recreation, though the New England common was an open grass area in the middle of towns or villages, originally used as common pasture. Later it was often used for various forms of recreation such as ball games, skating on the pond, fishing in the river, and watching the parades. We have inherited these practical attitudes and values and this is why it is often hard to achieve an appropriate rhythm between leisure and work in our lifestyle of today. "We must, under any circumstances, try to deal intelligently with the problems of leisure. If we do learn how to use leisure to cultivate our minds, hands, and hearts, we shall preserve and strengthen human values as well as make leisure contribute to the order, rather than the disorder, of life."[4] In the early part of the Industrial Age the factory worker laboured long hours and had little leisure in his daily life. In 1840 a man worked 84 hours a week while 100 years later Man only works 40 hours. With industrialization the growth of cities propelled us into a life of mechanization and specialization. Many new immigrants of different ethnic backgrounds arrived on our shores and brought with them their interests, such as the Germans who brought with them their "Turnverein" and emphasis on health-giving gymnastics.[5]

Organized popular sports and games in the early part of the nineteenth century became most popular; theatres, circuses, amusement parks, and children participated in these leisure time activities with their families and friends. While the Industrial Revolution helped to reduce Man's actual hours at work, free him from toil, and give him luxuries unknown to him, it brought the problems of crowded cities, with ill health and crime.

Man, however, has over all living creatures a unique attribute—he can change the environment and thus, out of the dire need to change the city into a better and healthier place to live, the Playground Movement was born in the latter part of the nineteenth century, guided by citizens who first realized that every individual has a right to exercise and play. "Play is as necessary to a child as food, and in a city where every square foot of ground has a market value a place to play must be supplied by the city, because otherwise the children convert streets into playgrounds, to their own harm and the annoyance and danger of adults who use the streets for business or pleasure."[6]

The birth of the first playground was in Boston and it opened in 1887. It was a sand garden for children five to ten years old. Dr. Marie Zakrzewska took the initiative to write a letter to the Massachusetts Emergency and Hygiene Association stating that she had seen such sand gardens in Berlin—she urged that Boston should build these, for sand play was necessary for all children.[7] Later many sand playgrounds were incorporated in Boston's parks and school systems and the idea spread to other cities.

In 1889 the first public outdoor gymnasium and playground for both girls and boys and for all ages, was opened on the banks of the Charles River in Boston, through the efforts of a citizen organization called the Massachusetts Emergency and Hygiene Association. This outdoor gymnasium featured the first iron jungle gym, designed by Dr. Dudley Sargent

of Harvard University,[8] who had remembered
what he liked as a child which, in designing
playgrounds, is most important. It had teeter-
totters, swings, climbing ropes, poles, and running track with grass in the centre to tumble on,
and sheltered seats for mothers to sit and watch.
It was all surrounded with beautiful flowering
shrubs and tall bushes, and laid out by the firm
of Frederick Law Olmstead, the great landscape
architect whose work includes Central Park in
New York and Mount Royal in Montreal.

Most playgrounds contained from then
on standard equipment emphasizing the physical needs of boys and girls. "The playground
movement is one of the desirable ways through
which this demand can be met. Playgrounds,
meaning places for children to play, and
for older folks to rest, walk and ride, as well
as play, were comparatively numerous in some
cities two decades ago and more. But just a
place, just a lot of land open to public use, will
not answer the requirements. Experience has
taught this and re-taught it. There is play and
there is play. There is play that grows like a
weed and never gets beyond the weed state; and
there is play that has careful cultivation so that
it becomes a useful plant. The latter kind is
required to accomplish results worthy of efforts
expended. This is the kind that all wise investi-
gators and expert students contend for, as soon
as they get far enough into the subject to truly
appreciate practical conditions."[9]

Supervised play by trained and salaried
leaders was aspired, and guidelines were laid

down for their training in pedagogy in special schools and colleges, and desirable characteristics of a teacher were defined. "President [Theodore] Roosevelt expressed the idea as applied to playgrounds in these words:

> "Neither must any city believe that simply to furnish open spaces will secure the best results. There must be supervision of these playgrounds, otherwise the older and stronger children occupy them to the exclusion of the younger and weaker ones; they are so noisy that people living in the neighborhood are annoyed; they are apt to get into the possession of gangs and become the rendezvous of the most undesirable elements of the population; the exercise and play is less systematic and vigorous when without supervision; and moreover in all cities where the experiment has been tried it has been found that such playgrounds are not well attended."[10]

Through these citizens' groups, social reforms occurred and cities realized that they could not grow haphazardly, but had to frame legislation for land acquisition for recreation. Cities such as Brookline, Massachusetts, voted funds for land acquisition as early as 1872, which unfortunately was never used. Eventually demands increased, and cities pushed the municipalities to include funds for playgrounds in their budgets. Finally in 1897 a law was passed to create such playgrounds for schools in New York City, including recreation space on roofs, and in 1899 the first municipal playground opened in New York.

In 1907 after the earthquake, San Francisco voted a bond issue of $741,000 for the purchase of playground sites and an appropriation of $20,000 for running expenses in 1908. A Playground Commission was established to carry this work out as part of the official municipal government structure. These were hopeful signs; yet the crowded cities were full of inhabitants with little space for play, and citizens agitated for legislation to make it a mandatory requirement to adopt space standards of 30 square feet per child on school playgrounds arguing that "The children's playgrounds rightly belong to the city. It is provident work and is far less costly than the reformatory and the juvenile court."[11] These citizens argued that playgrounds need not be large spaces, and play should take place on empty lots, waste places, and rooftops or piers. (I hope this sounds familiar to us in the 1970s.)

By 1898 there were twenty-four playgrounds open in the schools, open to the public after hours. In remodelling one of the buildings of the Roosevelt Hospital in the summer of 1908, provision was made for a roof playground for children in this institution. In fact, charity workers agitated that a law be passed in New York City that tenement houses should have walls 3' 4" above the roof line on all sides so that this space might be made into a safe place for children's play. (This Le Corbusier did in his building in Marseille some fifty years later.[12])

And we are trying to make buildings in our cities more useful for all sorts of activities today.

The idea of building playgrounds spread last, but not least, also to Canada. It was in the Province of Ontario in 1883 that the first Canadian legislation was passed to enable municipal parks to be developed, called the Provinces Public Parks Act. In 1888 Port Arthur adopted the Public Parks Act and established a Parks Board of Management in accordance with the Act; slowly, other towns followed such as Ottawa and later Toronto. For example, in Ottawa, City Council voted in 1898 to set aside eleven lots for recreation purposes and this became known as the Ottawa Ward Playground. The Mayor at this time agreed to improve and equip the grounds at no expense to Council. And this again shows us that the local Council of Women had to do most of the work in order to obtain places for children to play. This led to the founding of the Ottawa Playground Association in 1913, and the development of supervised playgrounds several years later. The first supervised playground in Halifax opened in 1906 under the guidance of a Miss Ford of the Hyannis School in Boston. In 1912 the first supervised playground was operated in Vancouver at MacLean Park.

In Toronto most of these playgrounds were in the school system and were supervised by trained leaders who worked according to the following concept that "The supervision of play does not mean domination of the children nor intermeddling in the decision of children in regard to their play. The teacher in charge is the senior partner of the children to adjust differences, to plan the general management of the grounds so that all may have the opportunity to play without interfering with the right and privileges of others."[13] Many Torontonians were not satisfied with the School Board playgrounds operated only during the vacation period, and therefore formed in 1910 the Toronto Playground Association. This organization pressed the Parks Department to establish playgrounds on city property, which the association would run. The first such co-operative playground opened in 1909 and was called St. Andrew's Square; it was in a densely populated neighbourhood 2½ acres large, with apparatuses for boys and girls such as see-saws, outdoor circle swings, sand boxes and gymnastic equipment, rope ladders, and trapezes. Later in 1912 this playground was turned over to the newly formed Parks Department.

In Montreal, through the interest of the Council for Women, playgrounds were built on the Boston "Sand Garden" model on vacant lots and other suitable places. Miss Ellen Tower of the Massachusetts Emergency and Hygiene Association played a major role in establishing these. In 1904 the Parks and Playground Association was formed with the sole purpose of "Promoting the preservation and extension of the parks and open spaces in and about the city of Montreal, the provision of children's playgrounds, the improvement of the city, the acquisition of land and other property to be used for the benefit of the citizens of Montreal for the purposes of recreation and other similar purposes in and about Montreal and other parts of the Province of Quebec."[14] In the summer of 1904 five properly supervised playgrounds were open. They were attended by 30,000 children which gave rise to concern because of overcrowding, so that in 1906 a resolution was passed by the Association: "Our aim has been to have several playgrounds scattered through the city so as to have an object lesson as to the needs of the children in the summer in each section of the city. In this we have been partly successful, and the large attendance of children has demonstrated their wishes. We feel that a good beginning has been made, but we look for much better results … We think it has proved itself to be the work of civic value, and one that should be eventually undertaken by the city, as its full development would be too large a tax on private effort."[15]

The interest in playgrounds was growing steadily. In 1912 McGill offered a playground leadership training course, running for seven hours per week for 15 weeks. The curriculum, under the guidance of Ethel Cartwright, contained courses in: educational psychology, psychology of play, practical conduct of playgrounds, kindergarten games, songs, storytelling, anatomy, first aid, games, athletics, manual work, and folk dancing. This was a farsighted programme indeed—one which we could well use today.

We have reached therefore a very important point in the early part of the twentieth century, with citizens' groups agitating for municipal legislation regarding land acquisition and staffing of playgrounds. In 1906 the National Recreation Association was formed in New York, setting out in its charter the importance of acquiring sufficient land for play and recreation in our cities. From these few examples of creating playgrounds in the nineteenth century, it is evident that these social reformers who founded the playground movement had goals in mind (not too different from ours), namely to achieve:

1   Health through physical exercise.

2   Mental health through relaxation and play.

3   Educate the whole person based on influential philosophers of the past and have their ideas accepted by every municipality, which was no mean task.

Who then formulated these ideas for play?

The cult of the child began with Rousseau out of his own sinister guilt and conflicts with respect to procreation. In his work, he achieved a fresh view of the relationship and essentially, his views were sound from his preachment to mothers: "nurse your infants" to his conception that a life of activity within a simple, natural environment was the best accompaniment to a child's normal growth. Up to this point, children had been little men and little women and only slowly did parents begin to realize that they too had to have a life of their own.

No other book influenced education more than *Emile* by Jean-Jacques Rousseau (1712–1778), who realized that children must be educated by the mother, for she can play the most important role in the education. He found that it was most important to educate Man close to nature, and to gain an understanding of objects that he comes in contact with. However, Rousseau did not recognize that the child, through play, can learn and formulate ideas and recognize facts. It took a while longer until Johann Heinrich Pestalozzi (1746–1827) laid the foundations of modern elementary education. He wrote that the most important period in the child's development is from birth to the end of his first year. To recognize this was indeed a great step in the right direction. In his autobiography, *Swan Song*, he tried to express all his ideas on education. He wanted the lower classes to improve their way of life by having them understand what their children were studying; he stressed learning about life around them, and using their minds. He was against learning by rote and therefore emphasized understanding. He believed that one should train the senses and promote learning by children's self-activity and contact with nature. Never, in all his writing, did he mention play as we would mention it today; instead, he spoke of the child's "occupation."

Pestalozzi's student was Friedrich Froebel (1782–1852), who came from Germany to Switzerland to study with Pestalozzi. He created the kindergarten and abstract play equipment for it. His life was not easy, for there was great opposition to his concepts. In 1840 the doors of the first kindergarten opened in Bad Blankenburg, in Thuringia. Here, Froebel combined his educational ideals by gathering farmers' children together in a little house and giving them colourful paper, building blocks and other commonplace items, and told them: "Do with these whatever your soul desires, form your desires and thoughts into objects with which you can play. Play and become good and understanding human beings through play." The house opened into the garden where most interesting geometric shapes such as cylinders, tubes, balls were placed for the enjoyment of the children; today we would say they were abstract elements. Froebel's discourse on the *Education of Man* (1826) documents that play is never nonsense, but an important occupation which comes from within, and to confuse play with idleness is something which even we, in our century, still have to undo. In his writings, Froebel detailed play areas for boys and for girls—for girls he thought they would like to play in separate rooms or in intimate corners in the living room. Boys, on the other hand, should have a big playground and every community should create one so that boys could come together and interact with each other. He recognized the effects of play in the psychological and social sense and as an effective educational tool. The first playground, as we think of it in the modern sense, was Froebel's kindergarten. Froebel's ideas of child development were premature and against the prevailing social and economic customs of his day. In fact, in Prussia, kindergartens were forbidden for ten years from 1851 to 1861.

In the nineteenth century, in spite of efforts against child labour by people such as Robert Owen, a vast majority of children had to work because there was no minimum age to limit child labour. In many European countries and in some parts of the United States until World War I, children worked in the coal mines, as well as cotton and textile work; children in the country had to work on the farm; in contrast, children of the rich were raised as miniature adults. Only after child labour laws were passed—in England in 1819 and in the United States federally in 1916—was children's labour regulated.

If Froebel gave us the first kindergarten in 1840, it was [Carl] Theodor Sørensen, the famous Danish landscape architect, who gave us the first true Adventure Playground. He noticed that children seemed to prefer "junk" on building sites, developing their own brand of play with waste objects that they found there, and with great perception and courage he started the first "Scrammellegepladsen" in 1943 at Emdrup in a housing estate outside of Copenhagen, with a most talented leader. Lady Allen of Hurtwood visited this playground at Emdrup; she was so impressed by it that she started adventure playgrounds in England after the war. In her book, *Planning for Play*, she writes: "Adventure playgrounds are places where children of all ages can develop their own ideas of play [...] In these playgrounds their love of freedom to take calculated risks is recognized and can be enjoyed under tolerant and sympathetic guidance."[16] In Europe these ideas are on firm footing. In North America we have not yet freed ourselves completely from the more rigid and formalistic ideas of the early part of the century.

In 1966 the *New York Times* reports of Lady Allen's visit there: she commented on the frightful state of playgrounds in North America where there is nothing else except safe play on metal swings and slides and teeter-totters; she urged parents "to put in a claim against city fathers for emotional damage to their children because they failed to provide stimulating and exciting playgrounds for them."[17] Yes, we still have to do this—we have to prod our elected officials daily to remind them of the right of the child for a space for creative play—we have to teach parents and we have to teach designers to think not in abstract terms, but in human terms so that our playgrounds will be truly places for play commensurate with the needs of a conserver society. Therefore we should take a good look at our cities, not to ask for acquisition of new land or more land, but we should look at our cities from the point of view:

1   Where are the spaces that we can make more useful for our children?

2   How can we make these meaningful in terms of our educational goals?

3   How can the whole community be
     involved in this great task that lies
     ahead in our future?

so that a six-year-old does not have to send
a letter to me stating: "our present playground
isn't that bad, but after a year or more you
just run out of games and you get bored." This
demonstrates that there are not enough manipulative parts on the playgrounds, nor a leader
who guides in moments of frustration.

In order that we can achieve this fabric
of play, as I call it, throughout our cities, I
think we should all look at our cities and assess
vacant lots that could be used temporarily or
seasonally, or rooftops that could fulfill a useful
play function in a crowded neighbourhood or
look at our own backyard. We should investigate
into portable equipment and we certainly need
a little hardware, but more peopleware. It might
be that teachers who were unable to find work
in the school systems because of declining
population, could be employed year-round as
leaders on playgrounds in our cities. Now we
must move away from the rigid outdoor recreation space standards which were established
and campaigned for by the National Recreation
Association from 1906 onwards. These standards, though very helpful in the early part of
the century, gave us the rigid, traditional,
metallic playground of one acre per 1,000 population. Today, we need to reimport the country
into the city and an update to these [spaces].
The International Play Association published

the Malta Declaration, the Swiss, through Pro Juventute, prepared the Charter by Dr. [Alfred] Ledermann as far back as 1958.[18] These, as well as many other groups, such as the Task Force on Play of the Canadian Council on Children and Youth, are trying today to update spaces for play in our cities with a new set of guidelines for incorporation into our municipal structure today.

Since Expo '67 in Montreal and the demonstration of the Children's Creative Centre at the Canadian Federal Pavilion there are signs that we are building more suitable places for our children. In Vancouver, many schools and parks in the last five years have changed their spaces to a more natural look. With deeper understanding of "play" the work/leisure cycle in our lives becomes more intertwined. Play becomes a prerequisite for life itself. Dean Emeritus Neville Scarfe, of the University of British Columbia, said recently: "Play is the principal business of childhood. It is the way a child learns what no one can teach him. It is a bulwark of mental health. Within its self-imposed structure children set up and resolve challenges and conflicts that are physical, intellectual and social in nature."[19]

The difference between the historic experience with play and the antecedents of the recreative value of leisure lie in the fundamental changes of society itself. Time to play for young or old gradually emerged as a by-product of working and sustaining a surplus of food and other material goods, beyond mere survival.

As Man moved out of the cave and gathered in settlements, time and opportunity for recreation and play occurred. Often their leisure activities were tied to religious rituals and were the privilege of the "ruling" class. Play was a non-productive activity available only to those who could afford it by their position in the community or by their surplus assets.

In a nutshell, it was a luxury denied the poor or the slave, reserved for the wealthy, powerful, and the victor.

Since the French and American Revolutions and particularly as a consequence of the Industrial Revolution, play of the young and recreation for adults has become an individual's right and society's goal.

Perhaps the most obvious example of this trend is the trade union movement's growing insistence on negotiating increased "fringe benefits"—mostly more holidays and shorter work week in lieu of just more money. Beyond the annual paid holidays and early retirement, we have all become very familiar with the extra statutory holiday—now *one per month* as a right of employment across North America.

While more time off work creates the opportunity for old and young, we have not yet translated these social opportunities into the activity pattern of the city and its play spaces. Therein lies our immediate challenge.

While young and old have more time—where can they exercise these choices? It will be essential to design more challenging and more flexible play and activity spaces as our cities become more compact and mature. This will be a complex and professionally demanding task in the next decade for two reasons:

1   A declining birth rate and an aging population will present special and new demands on where and how play will occur.

2   A stable or declining population committed to an efficient and conservative economy will provide less capital funds for more land or building construction.

Both these constraints will demand:

i   multiple use of space and recreation facilities, for young and old,

ii integrating "leisure" activities into other productive activities within the built-up areas of cities and towns.

The history of the playground has a long past in intellectual terms and only a while ago has it come to fruition. By recognizing the child's right to play and the necessity of the adult to recreate, we must now make it a fully integrated function of modern life, not as the luxury of the future, but as a true fulfillment of a democracy and Man's self-realization.

Notes

1   United Nations' Declaration of the Rights of the Child (1959), principle 7.

2   Editor's note: This appears to be a reference to Andreas Ryff (1550–1603), a merchant, politician, and historian in Basel, Switzerland. In the transcript of the text for this lecture, it seems Hahn Oberlander has misrendered his last name as Rytt, and confused his birth year for the year of his autobiographical writings, which cease in 1574. Ryff's writings were not published until the nineteenth century.

3   Editor's note: Oberlander's draft misdated the letter 1766 and misquoted from it, or perhaps quoted from an erroneous or modernized edition. The letter is from 2 June 1777 and reads: "I Love to recieve Letters very well much better than I love to write them, I make but a poor figure at Composition my head is much too fickle, my Thoughts are running after birds eggs play and trifles, till I get vexd with my Self, Mamma has a troublesome task to keep me Steady, and I own I am ashamed of myself. I Have but Just entered the 3d volume of Smollet [*A Complete History of England*] tho I had designed to have got it Half through by this time. I have determined this week to be more diligent as Mr. Thaxter will be absent at Court, and I cannot persue my other Studies I have Set myself a Stent, and determine to read the 3d volume Half out, If I can but keep my resolution I will write again at the end of the week, and give a better account of myself. I wish sir you would give me Some instructions with regard to my time and advise me how to proportion my Studies and my Play, in writing and I will keep them by me and endeavour to follow them."

4   Charles K. Brightbill, *The Challenge of Leisure* (Englewood Cliffs, New Jersey: Prentice Hall, 1960).

5   Editor's note: "Turnverein" are gymnastics clubs.

6   Everett B. Mero, ed., *American Playgrounds: Their Construction, Equipment, Maintenance and Utility* (Boston, MA: American Gymnasia Company, 1908), 37.

7   Marie Zakrzewska (1829–1902), Polish-born physician and educator, who founded the New England Hospital for Women and Children to train women as physicians and nurses. It opened in Boston in 1862.

8   Editor's note: Dudley Allen Sargent (1849–1924), US educator and proponent of physical activity.

9   Mero, *American Playgrounds*, 17.

10   Mero, *American Playgrounds*, 39.

11   Mero, *American Playgrounds*, 55.

12   Editor's note: This is a reference to Unité d'Habitation.

13   Elsie Marie McFarland, *The Development of Public Recreation in Canada* (Canadian Parks/Recreation Association, 1970), 27.

14   McFarland, *Development of Public Recreation in Canada*, 21.

15   McFarland, *Development of Public Recreation in Canada*, 22.

16   Editor's note: Lady Allen of Hurtwood (Marjorie Allen), *Planning for Play* (London: Thames and Hudson, 1968), 55.

17   Editor's note: see Charles L. Mee Jr., "Putting the Play in Play," *New York Times*, November 6, 1966.

18   Editor's note: This sentence appears to refer to the 1977 *Declaration of the Child's Right to Play*, produced by the International Play Association at their meeting in Malta, and to Pro Juventute, a charitable organization dedicated to the needs of Swiss children.

19   Editor's note: This appears to be a misattribution, or Oberlander cites Scarfe's quotation of Dorothy Cohen, *The Learning Child* (New York: Pantheon Books, 1972), 337.

Planning for Play Everywhere

> Every child should have mud pies,
> grasshoppers, water-bugs, tadpoles, frogs,
> mud-turtles, elderberries, wild strawber-
> ries, acorns, chestnuts, trees to climb,
> brooks to wade, water lilies, woodchucks,
> bats, bees, butterflies, various animals to
> pet, hay fields, pine cones, rocks to roll,
> sand, snakes, huckleberries, and hornets;
> any child who has been deprived of these
> has been deprived of the best parts of
> his education.[1]
> — Luther Burbank (1848–1926, US botanist)

Spaces for exploring are needed and not the
pocket-handkerchief-size playground with its
rigid structures.

Let the child determine how it wants to
use the space. A play space for the child indoors
or out must be a place that is large enough for
the activities of a three- to five-year-old, as well
as older age groups. Play starts the moment the
mother opens the door, and play does not stop
when the door is closed. Play is a part of the
infrastructure of living and this possibility for
play should be built into the total environment.
Play spaces are for socializing, communicating,
exploring, and sharing. Parents and the community have to learn to identify the needs of

the child as to learning, playing, and acquiring skills. The spaces for this development of the child can be linear/non-linear, such as a lane or a backyard, small/large, flat/sloped, wooded/ open. They must be safe, and readily convertible, as the needs and age structure of the household or the community change.

Seymour Gold observed in his article called "Non-Use of Neighborhood Parks"[2] that there are serious implications of the non-use of expensive areas, and thereby he challenges the wisdom of continuing to acquire and build neighbourhood parks which are so often neglected, because the residents have not been involved in the planning, construction, maintenance, and ongoing evaluation.

Paul Davidoff goes further in urging citizens to be involved on a sustained basis in all phases of the planning, design, management, and decision-making process, and with all citizens, it means involving the child in planning his or her places to play.[3]

As far back as 1970, in a book written by Jeannette Galambos Stone and Nancy Rudolph for the National Association for the Education of Young Children, we can read:

> Children, of course, make their own playgrounds everywhere. They practice stunts and use their physical prowess in throwing and jumping rituals ... They thrust ahead in improvisations of running and hiding, skipping and chanting, playing ball and chalk games in the street, balancing,

climbing trees and telephone poles, or
putting together a dollhouse or clubhouse
from cloth and sticks in the back yard.
They try out new ideas, establish rules, discuss ways and means, try, fail, try again.[4]

Imagination, creativity of the child, therefore
does not need a specially designated neighbourhood space. In studying children of all ages, one
can readily see how "they used space and materials in their play. But as we progressed and our
insights sharpened, we found increasingly that
we could not separate the concepts of learning-
through-play from the life-styles of whole neighbourhoods. And so we came to feel that to treat
playgrounds as separate entities, unrelated to
anything else in the community, is to repeat the
mistakes of a generation now past."[5]
    Therefore let us, in the era of a conserver
society, re-think our cities and ask ourselves
the following questions:

1   How can we, in our urban areas,
    satisfy this instinctive desire to play?

2   Ask any parent, what would you like
    to do inside your house or apartment?

Therefore the community should demand an
environment where the fabric of play permeates
our cities. Based on this premise, the community
should get together and plan space needs for
the child and *with* the child from 0 to 5, 6 to 8, 8
to 18, with three important ingredients in mind.

1   The Space
       Good play spaces indoors and out are
       a set of interrelated spaces for resting,
       thinking, learning, playing, and working.

2   The Leader
       A good leader may be a parent, a grand-
       mother, or a trained teacher. He or she
       must be a resourceful person with infinite
       patience and understanding of children's
       needs. Must be able to develop trust
       amongst the children and the neighbour-
       hood. The leader must be responsible as
       well as an enthusiastic person.

3   Cost Factor
       Remember we are approaching a
       Conserver Society. In the future, fewer
       playgrounds will be developed and
       play spaces will not be built by the
       Municipality or School Board without
       community effort and involvement. All
       those concerned that spaces for play will
       happen, and those who become involved,
       will get endless inspiration from the
       children. The community, when it has
       formulated its ideas, goals, etc., with the
       help of the children must call on techni-
       cally trained people, such as Architects,
       Landscape Architects, Engineers, to real-
       ize their ideas. Building a sandbox has a
       lot more to it than the finished product.

The accompanying chart is designed to help devise a process as well as a programme for your community to create spaces indoors and out for fulfilling play.

TAKE A LOOK AT:
YOUR HOME
YOUR BACKYARD
YOUR NEIGHBOURHOOD
FOR PLAY SPACES

If one takes a careful look at any neighbourhood, one will readily discover many sites which could be utilized for an exciting playing and learning environment. Potential sites undoubtedly exist in most urban, suburban, or rural areas. The following chart may be a guide in the initial planning process.

INVENTORY OF SPACES

Urban

Existing public park space
Religious or institutional properties
Urban plazas
Shopping centres
Street
Mall
Empty lot
Common lanes
Closed streets or back yards
Market places

School properties
Apartment sites
Roof tops
Balconies
Deserted industrial properties
Tax delinquent lots

Suburban

Community centre library
School site
Major open space corridors
Abandoned transportation or utility lines
Rights-of-way
Industrial parks
Residential areas
Church and hospital properties

Rural

Open fields
Wooded slopes
Deserted orchard, vineyard, farmstead,
   or pasture
Forest land
Wood lot
Conservation property
School property

GOALS

What goals can be achieved through play?

Physical skills—motor co-ordination
Language skills
Social graces—friends' co-operation
Courage
Creativity, art, crafts, music
Inventiveness
Individuality—self-respect
Responsibility towards others
Close to nature—investigate
Fun and laughter

Who can help improve your child's world?

Parks department
School boards
Libraries
Daycare services
Teachers
Major employers
Community groups
Planning department
Parents
CHILDREN THEMSELVES
Community workers
Technical school
Drafting services
Architects
Landscape architects
Botanical gardens
Tree nurseries

Where do the funds come from?

> Municipal funding
> Provincial grants
> Federal community improvement funds
>   and work grants
> "Hold your own fun fair with the children"
> Auctions
> Donation of material and labour by
>   interested parents and local companies

How do you transform your ideas into reality?

1   Call a meeting at the local school
    or community centre and have a film
    or slide show on recent examples.

2   Formulate your goals by making a
    program of what you want to achieve.
    Take a survey of what you have,
    what the children do, what is lacking
    for the children.

    Get children involved. Get approval
    from community and contact possible
    funding agents, or raise funds yourself.

3   Involve architect, landscape architect,
    engineers, and other technically
    competent people as facilitators
    towards realizing and building your
    environment economically and safely.

4   Build the desired spaces for play
    and evaluate with the users each year
    how to improve it.

THE SITE

Flat or sloping, must be well-drained—good exposure.

There are 7 ingredients for a good playground space.

1   Hills and dale

2   Sand and water

3   Trees, grass, and garden areas.

4   Storage area—magic box containing manipulative parts

5   Sheltered area from rain

6   Safe but challenging areas for swinging, climbing, and wheel toys

7   A good leader

Notes

1   Editor's note: Luther Burbank, *The Training of the Human Plant* (New York: The Century Co., 1907), 107.

2   Editor's note: Seymour Gold, "Nonuse of Neighborhood Parks," *Journal of the American Institute of Planners* 38, 6 (November 1972): 369–78.

3   Editor's note: Paul Davidoff (1930–1984), US urban planner, author, and community activist.

4   Jeanette Galambos Stone and Nancy Rudolph, *Play and Playgrounds* (National Association for the Education of Young Children: Washington, DC, 1970), 19.

5   Stone and Rudolph, *Play and Playgrounds*, 13.

This publication has been made possible by a grant awarded by the Graham Foundation for Advanced Studies in the Fine Arts.

Concordia University Press gratefully acknowledges the generous support of the Birks Family Foundation, the Estate of Linda Kay, and the Estate of Tanneke De Zwart.

The Canadian Centre for Architecture thanks the Estate of Cornelia Hahn Oberlander for its collaboration and continued support.

Cornelia Hahn Oberlander on Pedagogical Playgrounds
With an introduction by Jane Mah Hutton

Canadian Centre for Architecture
Concordia University Press

Editorial Group   Meredith Carruthers, Albert Ferré,
                   Natasha Leeman, Geoffrey Robert Little,
                   Ryan Van Huijstee, with Anaïs Andraud
                   and Matthew Kalil

Graphic Design   Sean Yendrys

Research   Gabrielle Doiron, Charles Gonsalves,
                  Thomas Molander, Susannah Wesley

Printed and bound in Germany by Gutenberg Beuys
Feindruckerei, Langenhagen.
Image processing: Max-Color, Berlin

This book is printed on Forest Stewardship Council certified
paper and meets the permanence of paper requirements
of ANSI/NISO Z39.48-1992.

Concordia University Press's books are available for free
on several digital platforms. Visit www.concordia.ca/press

For more information on CCA Publications,
visit www.cca.qc.ca/publications

First English edition published in 2023
10 9 8 7 6 5 4 3 2 1

978-1-988111-37-7 Paper
978-1-988111-38-4 E-book

Title: Cornelia Hahn Oberlander on pedagogical play-
grounds / with an introduction by Jane Mah
   Hutton.
Names: Oberlander, Cornelia Hahn, author. | Hutton, Jane
Elizabeth, 1976- writer of introduction.
Description: Series statement: Building arguments |
Includes bibliographical references.
Identifiers: Canadiana (print) 2022039931X | Canadiana
(ebook) 20220399360 | ISBN 9781988111377
   (softcover) | ISBN 9781988111384 (HTML)
Subjects: LCSH: Playgrounds—Design and construction. |
LCSH: Playgrounds—Equipment and supplies. |
   LCSH: Playgrounds—Social aspects. | LCSH:
Playgrounds—History. | LCSH: City planning.
Classification: LCC GV425 .O24 2023 | DDC
711/.558—dc23

Canadian Centre for Architecture
1920 rue Baile
Montréal, Québec H3H 2S6

Concordia University Press
1455 de Maisonneuve Blvd. W.
Montreal, Quebec H3G 1M8

Cornelia Hahn Oberlander (1921–2021) was a landscape architect and educator known for her designs for sites across North America, including the Children's Creative Centre at Expo 67, Robson Square in Vancouver (1978), the National Gallery of Canada (1988), the Northwest Territories Legislative Building (1995), the atrium of the New York Times Building (2002), as well as seventy playgrounds. She was a Companion of the Order of Canada.

Jane Mah Hutton is a landscape architect and associate professor at the University of Waterloo School of Architecture.